BUGABOO ROCK

ROCK

A Climber's Guide

BUGABOO ROCK

A Climber's Guide

Randall Green
&
Joe Bensen

The Mountaineers/Seattle

The Mountaineers: Organized 1906 ". . . to explore, study, preserve, and enjoy the natural beauty of the Northwest."

3 2 1 0
4 3 2 1

Published by The Mountaineers
306 Second Avenue West, Seattle, Washington 98119

Published simultaneously in Canada by Douglas & McIntyre, Ltd.,
1615 Venables Street, Vancouver, B.C. V5L 2H1

Manufactured in the United States of America

Edited by Jim Jensen
Route topos by Rebecca Walker
Maps on pages 14 and 23 by Nick Gregoric
Cover design by Barbara Bash
Book layout by Nick Gregoric
Cover photograph: Climbers ascend the Bugaboo-Snowpatch Col; Pigeon Spire in the background
Frontispiece: The ladder pitch on the approach hike to Kain Hut
All photographs by Joe Jensen and Randall Green

Library of Congress Cataloging in Publication Data

Green, Randall.
  Bugaboo Rock : a climber's guide / Randall Green & Joe Bensen.
    p. cm.
  Includes bibliographical references.
  ISBN 0-89886-233-7
  1. Rock climbing—British Columbia—Bugaboos—Guide-books.
2. Mountaineering—British Columbia—Bugaboos—Guide-books.
3. Bugaboos (B.C.)—Description and travel—Guide-books.
I. Bensen, Joe, 1949–   . II. Title.
GV199.44.C22B7435   1989
796.5′223′09711—dc20   89-77605
                                                          CIP

CONTENTS

Acknowledgments

Many people and many sources were of such tremendous assistance in producing this guide. First and foremost, we must acknowledge our debt to Robert Kruszyna and William Putnam for their fine guide to the Interior Ranges, South. That little volume has been in our packs since our first visit in 1980. J. F. Garden's beautiful book, *The Bugaboos*, was a valuable source of non-technical information. We are therefore grateful to be able to build upon the work of earlier researchers.

Of the many individuals who helped us in our research, we are especially indebted to "Ranger Chris" Atkinson, Kain Hut guardian, climbing companion, and a bountiful source of information on climbing in the Bugaboos. From our initial investigations, right up to the final draft, Chris provided unstinting help and support for our project. He also provided valuable details for the topo diagrams in this guide. Rebecca Walker did an outstanding job on the topo diagrams.

Many climbers provided us with valuable first-hand information. We would especially like to thank Fred Beckey, Joe Buszowski, Peter Cole, Martin Conder, Hans Gmoser, Hugh Herr, Art Higbee, Bruce Howatt, Jon Jones, Layton Kor, Ward Robinson, Rob Rohn, Chic Scott, Daniel Vachon, and Colin Zacharias.

Thanks to B.C. Provincial Parks, and especially to Dennis Herman, Ron Rutledge, and John Walters for information concerning access and maps. The folks at the Archives of the Canadian Rockies, in Banff, were extremely helpful in making their fine collection available to us.

Finally, we would both like to thank Theresa DeLorenzo-Green for her support and understanding throughout this long process. Considering the many climbs she has done in the Bugaboos, she deserves recognition as an able "researcher" as well.

*This guide is respectfully dedicated to the greatest of **all** Canadian mountain guides, Conrad Kain, whose spirit resides in the Bugaboos for all time; and to Timmy the packrat, the blithe spirit who resides at the Bugaboo-Snowpatch Col.*

Conrad Kain's portrait in Kain Hut

INTRODUCTION

The Bugaboos

We envy anyone making their first visit to the Bugaboos. No group of peaks springs to the eye with more authority, more surprise, and more sense of great things to happen. You cannot see the spires from the outside world. They remain hidden from view, tucked neatly away in the rugged Purcell wilderness until that final turn of the road up to the trailhead parking area. Even after many visits, the sudden shock of that initial glimpse of Hound's Tooth, jutting grandly from the chaos of the Bugaboo Glacier, is still a tremendous thrill and a great joy.

And it just gets better, the higher you go. If the view from the bottom, looking up, is grand, then the vistas from the summits are spectacular. From the tops of these spires, the view spreads out below in unsurpassed magnificence—an encapsulated granite paradise, shut off from the rest of the world by range upon range of outlying peaks. This is a very special place.

Between the grand anticipation inspired by the views from below and the promise of even grander views from the summits, lies some extremely good climbing, and that is what this book is all about.

Early Exploration

In September 1910, climber/adventurer Thomas Longstaff and surveyor Arthur Wheeler led the first documented trip into the Bugaboos, accompanied by the young Canadian guide, Conrad Kain. They traveled by packtrain up Bugaboo Creek from the Columbia River, fording rushing tributaries and fighting mosquitoes as they followed a trail used by miners.

Prospectors had been exploring the rugged valley for years, culminating in 1906 with a small mining rush in the area near what is now Bugaboo Falls. Apparently, the name Bugaboo stemmed from the use of the word "bugaboo" by miners to describe a dead-end mineral lead.[1]

But the Longstaff-Wheeler Expedition was not looking for minerals. They were seeking passage to the peaks known as the Spillimacheen Spires, and would explore the range on their way to the Duncan River. They were not sure Bugaboo Creek would lead them to their objective, but after a long journey on horseback, they were rewarded with a breathtaking view of an immense glacier that fed the north fork of the creek. They named it the Harmon's Glacier, which eventually became known as the Bugaboo Glacier.[2]

The spires were named the Nunataks by an early geological

survey party, which viewed them from Septet Ridge, to the southeast. Nunatak means peaks or mountains standing isolated, like
"islands in a sea of ice—fingers of granite or spires that seem to
pierce the sky."[3] Howser and Bugaboo spires were known simply
as the Nunataks, while Marmolata was known as Center Peak.
When more and more people began to visit and explore the summits of the group, more descriptive names were adopted.

First Climbs

Six years after his first visit, Kain extensively explored the upper neve of the Bugaboo and Vowell glaciers. He guided clients to
the summits of Rock Ridge, Howser Peak, and the North Tower of
the Howser Massif.[4] Unlike some guides of the day who were con-
tent to take their clients up "milk runs," Kain was interested in
difficult climbs. To Kain, mountaineering meant technical climbing.[5]

The North Tower of the Howser Massif was a case in point. The
smooth, compact granite was new to Kain's companions, but it
reminded him of the Chamonix Aiguilles, which he had climbed
as a young guide. Up to that point, Kain's experiences in Canada
had been solely on the loose, textured sedimentary rock more
characteristic of the Rockies. But Kain adapted quickly, giving
the team the first ascent of the highest tower in the area as well
as introducing climbing techniques never before seen in Canada.

After Howser, the most appealing summit was Snowpatch
Spire, but since Kain deemed it "unclimbable," attention was
turned to Bugaboo Spire.[6] With Albert and Bess MacCarthy and
John Vincent, Kain set his sights on the South Ridge. They found
it relatively easy until a final obstacle blocked their passage only
a few hundred feet from the summit. A sharp gendarme with
sheer 1000-foot drops on either side seemed to be a "veritable
bugaboo," as MacCarthy later referred to it.

Kain attacked it directly, boldly leading the steep friction slab
without protection. Easier climbing then led to the South Summit. For years, the gendarme pitch, at 5.5 or 6.6, was considered
the hardest rock pitch in North America, and Kain is known to
have referred to Bugaboo Spire as his most difficult Canadian ascent, more difficult than his heralded routes on Mt. Robson.[7]

Climbing in the Bugaboos

All the climbing here, easy or difficult, is superb. The highly
crystalline granite is clean and hard, and the lines are steep,
long, and everywhere in sight. Most of the routes in the Bugaboos
follow cracks, dihedrals, and flake systems.

Yosemite-style big wall climbers will feel right at home in the
Bugaboos, as will veterans of the long classic rock routes in the

Climbers and park ranger Chris Atkinson dry gear in the sun at Kain Hut.

West Alps. Indeed, if any place in North America has the potential for becoming another Chamonix, surely this is it. On Bugaboo routes, one has the constant feeling of high solitude, a sort of Olympian detachment from the world below.

Next to the quality of the rock and the length of the routes, it's the scenery as much as anything that makes Bugaboo climbing such a treat. The West Ridge on Pigeon Spire is a low commitment run-up, something to do when the weather is marginal, and you don't want to hang around the hut. Yet it is one of the most beautiful climbs in the entire Bugaboo group, and in its own laid-back way, it is one of the most enjoyable. The views from the West Ridge—out onto the Howsers and back across a seemingly limitless panorama of outlying ranges—are nothing short of spectacular.

Perhaps the only drawback to climbing in the Bugaboos is the weather, which is often wretched. Not only is the season very short—from mid-June until the start of September—but there is just no telling whether you'll even get out of Kain Hut. Nature cuts loose here with unbridled enthusiasm and total disregard for the recreationalist.

One nice thing about the weather, however, is that it is fairly predictable. You can count on it clouding over and storming in the afternoon, so seasoned Bugaboo climbers adhere to the tradition of predawn alpine starts. And you usually can count on the weather coming out of the west. Of course, these considerations are not much help on routes that can't be completed by noon or those that face east.

Fortunately, unless you're attempting something extremely ambitious, it is possible, though usually not easy, to rappel most of the routes, then run like rabbits for the security of the hut. Yes, the weather can be brutal up here. Sometimes the weather will be off for a week straight, and if that's the week you drove up from way south of the border for your first Bugaboo holiday, it can be discouraging. As pleasant as the Kain Hut is, that's not where you want to spend an entire week. But when the weather is good in the Bugaboos, it's hard to imagine a better place to be.

It is doubtful that overcrowding will ever become much of an issue in the Bugaboos. There is plenty of rock, and as more routes are established there should be ample amusement for everyone. This area is far enough away from any major city that it may never have a truly "local" crowd of climbers. And with a stiff approach and uncooperative weather, visits to the Bugaboos will continue to be relatively serious undertakings.

There is very little alpine-style mixed climbing here. This is rock climbing in an alpine setting, with the snow and ice merely for ambience; you can probably leave your technical ice tools behind. You will want an ice axe and mountain boots for some of the approaches and returns, but even crampons are of debatable value. There is one technical ice route in the Bugs, the Big Hose on the South Tower of Howser Massif, but it is almost never in condition.

Some routes, such as Bugaboo Spire's Northeast Ridge, can be done hut and back in a pair of lightweight boots, but sticky shoes are standard Bugaboo climbing footwear. We consider an ample selection of chocks and nuts, a few camming devices, and lots of slings to be a standard rack for climbing in the Bugaboos. For the more gymnastic grades, two sets of Friends, small camming devices, and an ample supply of small nuts and slings are also recommended. On the longer routes that have had few ascents, it would be prudent to carry some pitons for fixing emergency rappel stations. An extra lightweight rope for rappels and emergency situations may be helpful, and helmets are recommended.

Inexperienced Bugaboo climbers often underestimate the time it takes to climb the spires. The dimensions of the area dictate that climbers must commit to multipitch routes. These spires are big and once you get started you just have to keep rolling or plan to bivouac. The Ministry of Parks recommends that all climbers carry a daypack with rainwear, extra warm clothing, and food. Only experienced climbers, practiced in crevasse rescue and properly roped, should venture onto the snowfields and glaciers. Climbers are responsible for their own safety, and rescue services are not readily available.

The Ministry of Parks also requests that climbers check with park rangers before departure. A register is kept in the Conrad Kain Hut for this purpose and your convenience. The park rangers are pleased to offer assistance or other information. In addition, the park rangers are climbers and alpinists who have a clear understanding of climbers' needs and concerns. They also maintain a climbing scrapbook containing interesting trivia and climbing route information. Pioneers of new routes are encouraged to share route descriptions and route information, so the scrapbook can be updated for future reference.

There are no established sites for the hard-core crag rat. The McTech area is as close as you'll find; there are slightly more than a half-dozen established climbs there, but only one is more difficult than 5.10. Of course, there is plenty of potential for more routes in the McTech area, as well as on nearby Eastpost Spire.

As for longer routes, few of the harder ones go completely free. It is fairly common for a route to go free to 5.10 +, then have some aid. There are a bunch of tremendous 5.10-plus-a-little-aid lines that will go free at 5.11 or 5.12. That's the sort of thing there is so much scope for. The few established 5.11s will usually consist of a pitch or two at that grade mixed in among 6 to 16 pitches of 5.7 to 5.10.

Bugaboo Provincial Park/ Alpine Recreation Area

In 1969 the British Columbia Ministry of Parks and the Alpine Club of Canada (ACC) began working together to preserve the beauty and fragile alpine ecosystems of the Bugaboos. The B.C. Ministry of Lands, Parks, and Housing set aside a portion of the area, Bugaboo Glacier Provincial Park, which includes only the access trail and the immediate area around Boulder Camp (the popular camping spot). The remaining area, including all the major glaciers and spires, became part of the Bugaboo Alpine Recreation Area (fig. 1).

Previous efforts by the ACC to preserve the fragile Boulder Camp by erecting two fiberglass shelters met with disdain from many visiting climbers. Galen Rowell said, "In my humble

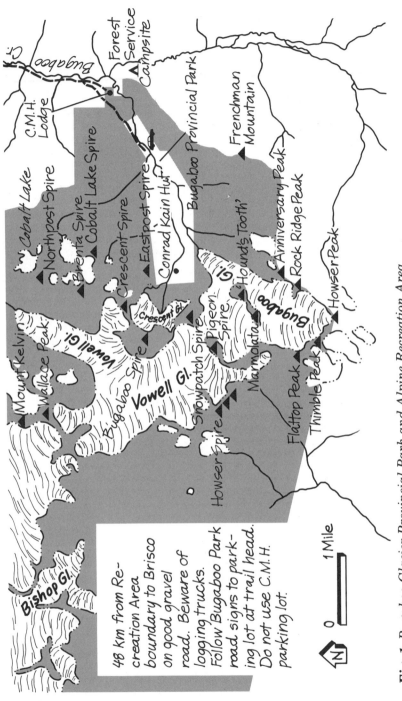

Fig. 1. *Bugaboo Glacier Provincial Park and Alpine Recreation Area*

Climbers lounge in Kain Hut during a spell of bad weather.

estimation it would be better to donate them to a construction company for use as outhouses."[8] It wasn't until the early 1970s that the construction of a large hut was proposed by the ACC. During the summer of 1972, the Conrad Kain Hut was erected by the ACC; the ugly plastic igloos were removed and parks personnel began to restrict visitor impact on the fragile timberline area below Snowpatch by limiting tent camping to designated areas only.

The Kain Hut sits on a bench at the foot of the moraine of the Crescent Glacier. It sleeps about 50 (though you probably wouldn't want to be one of the 50) and is comfortable to about 25. Although it is seldom full, the Ministry of Parks warns that visitors should not assume there will be room in the hut. In addition, hut accommodations are not available in winter due to avalanche dangers.

Overnight fees of $6.00 (Canadian) are assessed; running water, propane stoves, and lamps are provided. Sleeping bags, pads, and cooking gear are *not* provided. The rules of the hut are as follows:

• Boots are not to be worn in the hut; place them in the racks provided.
• Smoking is not permitted in the hut.
• Lighted candles are not permitted in the sleeping lofts.
• The use of personal stoves is prohibited.
• Stoves, sinks, and utensils are to be cleaned immediately after use.
• No noise between 10:00 P.M. and 7:00 A.M. Please respect the rights of other visitors who may be sleeping.
• Familiarize yourself with the location of fire extinguishers and emergency exits.
• Please use the sanitary facilities provided.
• Personal equipment and belongings must not be left without permission from the Park Ranger. An increasing number of thefts have been occurring; please be careful with your equipment.
• Occupancy is limited to 7 consecutive days and a maximum of 14 days in any year.

All in all, it's quite cozy. During bad weather there is nothing so pleasant as lying around in the upper loft of the Kain Hut, listening to the rain beat a wild staccato on the roof, looking out the window onto a bleak and miserable scene, and feeling so glad you're not up on one of those lightning-rod spires.

• • •

The notch between Bugaboo and Snowpatch spires (Bugaboo-Snowpatch Col) is one of the prominent physical features of the area, and the most important conduit of access for climbers and glacier skiers. This col divides the central Bugaboo Group into roughly eastern and western sectors.

The eastern sector includes the East faces of Bugaboo and Snowpatch, the Crescent Glacier, and the lesser summits of Eastpost, Brenta, Northpost, and the Crescents. The western sector consists primarily of the West faces of Bugaboo and Snowpatch, along with the peaks bordering the Vowell Glacier—Pigeon Spire and the Howser Massif.

There is, in addition, a more remote district of the Bugaboo Group, south of the major spires. Marmolata, Hound's Tooth, Flattop, Thimble, Anniversary, Rock Ridge, and Howser Peak are seldom visited, and almost entirely overlooked by climbers.

How To Use This Guide

Climbing information is of critical importance in a place like the Bugaboos, not only because of the number, length, and difficulty of the routes, but also because of the very serious nature of the objective hazards—glacier travel, stonefall, and fickle weather—as well as the difficulties of route-finding on big mountains. Yet detailed information on climbing in the Bugaboos has been sadly lacking. In addition to the short section in the Kruszyna-Putnam guide, the rest has been rather hit or miss— rough topos scrawled on torn bits of paper and loose anecdotes scribbled in the hut scrapbook. There are many fine climbs that appear to have been unknown to all but the first ascensionists and perhaps a handful of their friends fortunate enough to have learned of the line.

This guide was largely pieced together from those scraps of information and from phone calls and written follow-ups with climbers from across Canada and the U.S. We realize that we have missed some things. Without written documentation, it is difficult to keep track of the accomplishments of past climbers, and one cannot write a guidebook on hearsay. Some things are bound to go unrecorded, and are thus lost to future climbers.

Bouldering at Kain Hut

We hope that the information we have managed to accumulate will be of service to all who visit this outstanding area. We also hope that future first ascensionists will be prompted to leave detailed accounts of their climbs. The scrapbook in Kain Hut should serve as the on-going update to what has been collected here.

The individual sections of the introduction are designed to enhance the Bugaboo experience. The remainder of the book consists of climbing information. Peaks and spires are discussed individually to give some insight into their individual character, the story of the first ascent pioneers, plus detailed approach information for selected climbing routes. Climbing routes each have written descriptions for those who prefer this style of guide and who wish to maintain some sense of adventure. For those interested in more detailed information, topo-style line drawings are present for many of the more popular or difficult routes. (See fig. 2 for key to topo drawings.) In addition, marked photos show the general lines of ascent and descent on the major faces of most spires.

Appendices list chronological first ascents of each peak and spire, along with citations for our sources on each route. In addition, a table compares American (YDS and NCCS) to British climb ratings. The index helps you quickly locate your intended route by name or spire association.

Grading of Climbs

Several systems have been devised to indicate the difficulty and technical demands of rock climbing. Classifying climbing routes is highly subjective and may be affected by psychological and physiological factors, the type of rock, and how well it protects. These variables generally do not need to be considered when hill-walking or scrambling. However, Class 5 and Class 6 (aid) climbing may have a wide range of difficulty and technical demands. The rating system used in this guide is the widely known and accepted Decimal System, developed at Tahquitz Rock in central California in the early 1950s.

The six classes of climbing are as follows:

Class 1—Trail hiking.

Class 2—Hiking over rough ground like talus and scree that may include the use of hands for stability.

Class 3—Scrambling that requires the use of hands and careful foot placement.

Class 4—Scrambling over steep and exposed terrain using a rope.

Class 5—Serious climbing, demanding the use of a rope, protective hardware placements, and belays.

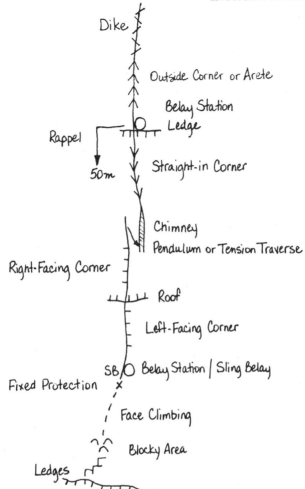

Dike

Outside Corner or Arete

Belay Station

Ledge

Rappel

50m

Straight-in Corner

Chimney

Pendulum or Tension Traverse

Right-Facing Corner

Roof

Left-Facing Corner

SB   Belay Station / Sling Belay

Fixed Protection

Face Climbing

Blocky Area

Ledges

lb.	Lieback	Thin	Thin crack (to 1½")
Chim.	Chimney	3RD	Class 3
OW	Off-Width	4th	Class 4
HB, RP	Very Small Chocks	KB	Knife Blade
TCU	Small Camming Devices	LA	Lost Arrow

Fig. 2. *Key to topo drawings*

Class 6—Aid climbing that calls for the use of anything other than the rock's natural features for support, progress, or rest. This category may be subdivided by the capital letter A (denoting aid) and a numeral from 0 to 5.

A0—Placements can be used for rest or to pull on for upward progress.

A1—Solid placements that can hold a fall; aid slings (etriers) are employed for ascent.

A2—Placements are more difficult to position, and they support less weight than those in the A1 category.

A3—Placements can hold a short fall only.

A4—Placements can support body weight only; long falls can occur.

A5—Enough A4 placements to risk a 50- or 60-foot fall.

In addition, an overall grade has been given to most routes in the form of a Roman numeral from I to VI. This rating refers to the degree of commitment, overall difficulty, ease of escape, and length of route. Grade I is represented by Class 4 scrambles, and easy Class 5 climbs that take only a few hours to complete. At the upper extreme, Grade VI climbs may take several days with a great deal of commitment in regard to difficulties, weather, and other objective dangers. Here are some examples of ratings: West Ridge (Pigeon Spire) II 5.4, or Warrior (North Tower of Howser Massif) VI 5.9/A3.

The Decimal System describes free-climbing difficulties in the Class 5 category; it begins with 5.0 (easiest) and follows mathematic logic to the 5.9 grade. When climbs harder than 5.9 were established, however, an open-ended rating system was adopted. Hence 5.10 (read five-ten) was introduced. Today, the rating scale has expanded to 5.14. Subgrades of a, b, c, and d have been added to climbs rated 5.10 and harder. These subgrades represent a finer comparison of technical difficulty than the more general + and − signs. However, some routes included in this guide have not received enough ascents to allow a consensus of opinion on their difficulty so the + and − sign will accompany the rating.

In cases where the ratings of routes in this guide are disputed, the upper grade has been chosen. Halfway up a Bugaboo route, it is better to find the climbing easier than expected. Climbers should use discretion when they are matching the rating of a route to their abilities. They should proceed with caution until they are familiar with the rock and have planned how to protect the climb.

Injuries sustained from falls are always possible, even on routes that can be well protected. Climbs included in this guide do not have a protection grade. A well-equipped leader should therefore be able to do a particular climb with a reasonable margin of safety. It might be wise for crag climbers without alpine experience to consider starting out on routes at least one to two grades easier than their maximum abilities.

Ethics and Environmental Considerations

These subjects have been discussed and argued at great length by most people who have participated in the sport of rock climbing. Rather than approaching the controversial issues, we will try to pass on the principles and ethics shared by most Bugaboo climbers. It may be argued that no one has the right to tell you how to climb. However, the sport (like society) needs some basic rules so that our actions will not adversely affect others or the environment we use.

It is common to encounter fixed protection on many routes. Bolts and pitons are maintained on several climbs where other "clean" types of protection were deemed impractical or unsafe by the first ascent party. The use of fixed protection and clean climbing methods helps preserve routes in their original condition for future generations of climbers.

Respect the fixed points of protection that have been left by previous parties. If you feel they inhibit your experience, you don't have to use them, but don't destroy or remove them. If you do use fixed protection, use caution. Natural elements may loosen placements, particularly in places like the Bugaboos where so much freezing and thawing occurs, so test fixed points before entrusting them with your life.

The Ministry of Parks reminds visitors that Bugaboo Glacier Provincial Park and Alpine Recreation Area belongs to the whole country. Please treat it with respect, and please help preserve and protect it.

Park rules include the following:

- Open fires are *not* permitted.
- Don't litter. Refuse should (we think, *must*) be carried out and disposed of properly. Animals searching for food dig up buried trash. If you respect the natural character of the land, pack out your trash.
- Flowers, shrubs, trees, and even rocks are part of the park's natural heritage. Please don't cut or damage them or remove them.
- The park's lakes and streams are the source of drinking water. Even "biodegradable" soaps will pollute water; so will food scraps. Help protect the delicate balance of the water system by washing yourself, your clothes, and your dishes at least 100 feet from lakes and streams.
- Dogs and other domestic pets are prohibited.

By following these rules, visitors can preserve the area's beauty for future generations to enjoy.

Safety

Climbing involves unavoidable risks that every climber must assume. The fact that a route is described in this book is no assurance that it will be safe for you. Routes vary greatly in difficulty and in the amount and kind of experience and preparation needed to enjoy them safely. Some routes may have changed or deteriorated since this book was written. Also, of course, climbing conditions can change from day to day due to weather and other factors. A route that is safe in good weather or for a highly conditioned, properly equipped climber, may be completely unsafe for someone else or under adverse weather conditions.

You can minimize your risks by being knowledgeable, prepared, and alert. There are a number of good books and public courses on climbing techniques and safety. Just as important, always be aware of your own limitations and the conditions existing when and where you are climbing. If conditions are dangerous or if you are not prepared to deal with them safely, change your plans.

Access and Camping

You will need a car to get to the Bugaboos. On Highway 95, 16.7 miles north of Radium Hot Springs, is a little logging community called Brisco. Here a Ministry of Parks sign marks the turnoff for the Bugaboo Recreation Area (see fig. 3). Turn left onto a good gravel road, open usually in late spring through late fall, that winds past a sawmill and crosses the Spillimacheen River.

At the West Side Road intersection follow small signs directing you to the Bugaboos. The road is about 28 miles (45 kilometers) long, winding through dense forest and climbing into a steep-sided valley. Heavy logging trucks travel this road during the week, so use caution on the narrow, blind corners. The views of the spires are obstructed until you get past Bugaboo Falls. Then follow a marked turnoff to the right, which leads to the Bugaboo parking area and trailhead. The main road continues another quarter-mile to Hans Gmoser's Canadian Mountain Holidays (CMH) Heli-ski Lodge, but parking here is restricted to lodge visitors only.

The Conrad Kain Hut can be seen from the trailhead parking lot, and the familiar Quonset shape appears to be an easy one-hour hike away. However, what looks like the typical small hut is actually much bigger, hence much farther away.

The trail is about three miles long and climbs 2133 feet as it follows the northern lateral moraine of the Bugaboo Glacier. In

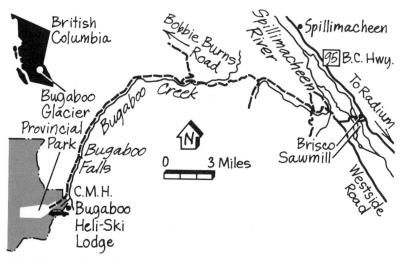

Fig. 3. *Bugaboo Alpine Recreation Area*

1984, the trail to the hut was completely overhauled. What was once a two-hour mini-epic of steep, back-breaking grades and hair-raising stream crossings is now a fairly mellow two-hour grind.

The Ministry of Parks recommends that strong, reliable footwear be worn and advises extreme caution along the steep path. For prolonged visits, with large packs full of climbing paraphernalia, food, beer, and a tent for placing high camps above the hut, it makes sense to do two lighter carries.

The Ministry of Parks restricts tent camping to designated areas on the terraces just below the hut and at sites on Applebee Dome. Outside the park and in the recreation area, camping is not restricted to specific sites. They recommend that bivouac sites be chosen carefully to prevent contamination of water sources and to minimize damage to alpine vegetation.

Notes

[1] J. F. Garden, *The Selkirks, Nelson's Mountains,* Footprint, (1985), 29.

[2] Eugene F. Boss, *Canadian Alpine Journal,* 59:38.

[3] J. F. Garden, *The Selkirks, Nelson's Mountains,* Footprint, (1985), 30.

[4] Robert Kruszyna and William Putnam, *Interior Ranges of Canada,* AAC, (1977), 79.

[5] Chris Jones, *Climbing in North America,* AAC, (1976), 81.

[6] Chris Jones, *Climbing in North America,* AAC, (1976), 80.

[7] *American Alpine Journal,* 1:297.

[8] Galen Rowell, *AAJ,* 18:62.

EASTPOST SPIRE

8850 ft. (2697 m)

Appearance and Location

A ridge on the southeastern flank of Eastpost descends from the summit (broken south slopes) to below the Conrad Kain Hut. The lower flanks of the SE Ridge form the rugged northern boundary of the park approach trail. The true S Face is a sheer 800-foot diamond-shaped headwall that is split in the center by a prominent dihedral formation.

At the base of the S Face is a slightly down-sloping, broken, rubble-strewn bench that extends toward the southwest to an adjacent granite outcrop called Applebee Dome. Applebee Dome's lower southern ramparts bar easy access to Eastpost from the south. Here the receding Crescent Glacier has deposited steep moraine ridges that bound a rushing stream, which cascades down along the southwest flank of Applebee Dome.

Above Applebee Dome, talus slopes extend from the Crescent Glacier tarns up and around the western flanks of Eastpost to a notch (Crescent-Eastpost Saddle) in the ridge that is connected to the Crescent Towers. From the notch, a short, steep, broken northwest ridge extends to the false summits northwest of Eastpost's main summit.

Beyond the northwest ridge notch, snowfields extend into a basin north toward Brenta and Cobalt Lake spires. On Eastpost's northern flanks, moderate snow slopes extend to the summit blocks. To the northeast, another prominent ridge-line descends from the summit to below the tree line.

Notable First Ascents

Eastpost reportedly was first climbed by Eaton Cromwell and F. S. North in August 1938. They crossed the Crescent-Eastpost Saddle and traversed the northern snow slopes to a notch in the NE Ridge. The upper NE Ridge was then climbed to the summit.

The first major technical route was established on Eastpost by Joy Kor and W. Sanders, who climbed the S Face route in July 1960.

Climbing Eastpost Spire

Excluding the S and W faces, most routes on Eastpost are nothing more than a scramble. The steep S and W faces offer a variety

View above Kain Hut; Applebee Dome on the left and Eastpost Spire on the right

of technical climbing opportunities. The rock is a lesser quality granite compared to the rest of the spires. Decomposing and granular, the rock is split by cracks that are often incipient, rounded and flared. Many short, free-climbing possibilities still exist on these faces, however. Due to the nature of the rock, take along a selection of pitons in addition to your normal rack for routes on the S Face.

Near the Crescent-Eastpost Saddle, an abundance of steep practice slabs offer superb top-rope climbs ranging from moderate Class 5 to 5.11. The rock is very rough and crystalline due to extreme weathering from prevailing winds that accelerate through the saddle. No permanent anchors exist, but cracks and bollards are abundant for rigging anchors. Loose rock near the top of the slabs may pose rockfall hazards, so use extreme caution and clear away loose rock before setting anchors. This area can be a pleasant diversion when storm clouds enshroud the spires or for practicing techniques needed to ascend some of the more demanding crack climbs on the big peaks.

In addition, Applebee Dome offers excellent bouldering and scrambling near the tenting area. On the southern flanks of Applebee (the face that descends toward the Kain Hut) many crack systems provide excellent climbing, though often wet and mossy. Many climbs have been done here, but very little has been recorded. Therefore, only one route for this area is included in this section.

Excluding the SE Ridge routes, most routes are approached by ascending the moraine trail to Applebee Dome. From Applebee, it is easy to approach the saddle area and S and W faces by skirting the glacier tarns and following faint trails up the talus and scree slopes on the southwestern flank. Cross the saddle for access to the easier slopes and routes on the northern flanks.

Route Descriptions

A   Northeast Ridge

II

Approach: Ascend moraine slopes above Applebee Dome to Crescent-Eastpost Saddle. Cross this rocky pass to gain snowfields on the north slopes of Eastpost. Ascend snowfields toward prominent col in NE Ridge. Scramble col to summit. **Time:** 2.5–3 hours from Kain Hut. **Descent:** Down-climb same route or NW Ridge.

B   Northwest Ridge

II   *(photo, p. 28)*

Approach: Same as for NE Ridge. At saddle, scramble block-strewn slabs to narrow ridge crest. Follow ridge crest and join NE Ridge. Scramble to summit. *Time:* 2.5 hours from Kain Hut. *Descent:* Down-climb same route.

C   East Face

Class 4

Approach: Same as for NE Ridge or traverse peak to the south and east from meadows above Kain Hut. Several easy scramble routes exist. A relatively long approach for little or no actual climbing. *Time:* 3 hours from Kain Hut. *Descent:* Down-climb same route or NW Ridge.

D   Upper Southeast Ridge

Class 4

Approach: Traverse southwestern meadows above Kain Hut to S Shoulder. Scramble easy terrain until upper rock ridge is easy to climb. Mostly a scramble. *Time:* 2 hours from Kain Hut. *Descent:* Down-climb same route or E Face.

E   Southeast Ridge Direct

II   5.5–5.6

Approach: Same as for Upper SE Ridge. Begin climbing at lowest point of rock. Ascend 200 feet of moderate Class 5 terrain along ridge. Scramble easy terrain (Class 4) on upper ridge to summit. *Time:* 2–3 hours from Kain Hut. *Descent:* Down-climb same route.

F   South Face

III   5.6/A2 *(photo, p. 28)*

Approach: Ascend Crescent Glacier moraine to Crescent-Eastpost Saddle. Traverse south along sloping ledges to base of broken section of main face. **1–2** Aid a series of long steep cracks. **3** Traverse right to large open book. **4–6** Follow rotten corner using some aid to just west of main summit. *Time:* 5–6 hours from Kain Hut. *Descent:* Down-climb NW or SE Ridge.

G   South Face-Left

III   5.7/A3

Approach: Same as for S Face. Route begins left of the S Face Route in a prominent dihedral. **1–2** Strenuous climbing leads to a sling belay below an overhang. **3** Aid past overhang and scramble to NW Ridge. Account is unclear, but two sling belays were used in only three pitches of Class 5 climbing. *Time:* 3–4 hours from Kain Hut. *Descent:* Down-climb NW or SE Ridge.

H   Shelton's Route West Face

II   5.10 *(fig. 4) (photo, p. 28)*

Approach: Same as for S Face. Start at the base of a short steep face that juts out of a large sloping bench that resembles an amphitheater. The route ascends a left-facing inside corner that begins near a large block that sits on the bench and leans against the wall. **1** Climb groove up and left below roof, mantle onto small sloping ledge below steep dihedral (20 feet). **2** Lieback corner to small belay at top of flake on right wall (60 feet). **3** Lieback, stem, and face climb corner to huge low-angle slab (65 feet). **4** Scramble corner of slab and headwall on right to NW Ridge. *Time:* 3–5 hours from Kain Hut. *Descent:* Down-climb NW Ridge to saddle.

I   West Face #2

II   5.8 *(photo, p. 28)*

Approach: Same as for Shelton's Route. Several hundred feet west of Shelton's Route is a groove in the W Face that starts at the top of a scree-and-talus cone. Route follows the groove to NW ridge crest at a large boulder with a cairn. First and last pitches are enjoyable Class 5 climbing, but quality is marred by piles of loose rock on low-angle ground in the middle section. *Time:* 2 hours from Kain Hut. *Descent:* Down-climb NW Ridge to saddle.

APPLEBEE DOME

Approach: From Kain Hut, ascend a steep trail on moraine ridges (Crescent Glacier) along southwest flanks of Applebee Dome to top of waterfall. At rocky bench just below the west side of Applebee, traverse boulder field and ascend short slope to north end of flat bench that forms top of Applebee Dome. A camping area with toilet facilities is established there. Drinking water sources are available from glacier tarns slightly higher to the north of the dome top.

Eastpost Spire, S and W faces

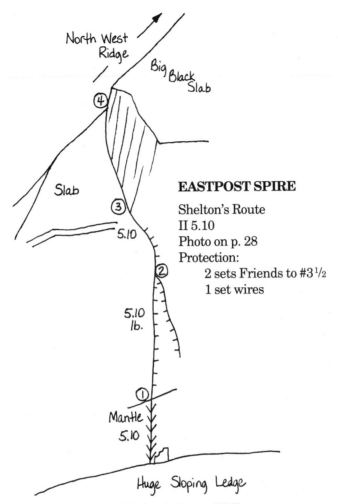

North West Ridge

Big Black Slab

④

Slab

EASTPOST SPIRE

③

5.10

Shelton's Route
II 5.10
Photo on p. 28
Protection:
    2 sets Friends to #3 ½
    1 set wires

②

5.10
lb.

①

Mantle
5.10

Huge Sloping Ledge

Fig. 4. *Eastpost Spire, Shelton's Route/W Face*

J   Dislocation

I   5.6

Approach: From Kain Hut, hike to base of Applebee's southern buttress. The route starts below the lowest point of Applebee's southern flank as seen from the Kain Hut. **1–3** Follow toe of smooth buttress for three pitches of crack system, which rises to the right. **4–5** Follow short traverse left to finish in large dihedral, which ends at the lowest scree slopes of Eastpost. ***Time:*** 4 hours from Kain Hut. ***Descent:*** Walk down Crescent Glacier moraine trail to hut.

COBALT LAKE SPIRE
8750 ft. (2667 m)

Appearance and Location

Cobalt Lake Spire is part of a large cirque, which is formed by three distinct summits and connecting ridge-lines. It stands on the easternmost edge of the cirque that encircles Cobalt Lake. The spire's rubble-strewn appearance makes it look as though it has been subjected to more of the destructive erosion that has shaped the peaks and spires of the Bugaboo Group.

Three ridges of decomposing granite descend from its summit: one toward the northeast, to the lake's outlet; another drops steeply to the southeast; the third extends due west toward Brenta Spire and connects to its S Ridge. Heavy black lichens cover most of the exposed rock, giving it a black and foreboding appearance. Although there are steep sections of rock, most of it is unsuitable for climbing.

Notable First Ascent

An Alpine Club group led by A. C. Faberge climbed the peak via the W Ridge during the summer of 1946. They followed what is now the popular Cobalt Lake Trail to where a saddle in the W Ridge meets Brenta Spire's S Ridge. From this point, they followed the blocky ridge to a 300-foot steep, rotten face. They climbed the face to where it joined the upper section of the N Ridge, which gave easy access to the summit.

Climbing Cobalt Lake Spire

Although its summit offers excellent views of Cobalt Lake, no quality technical climbing routes exist, to date. Its lower flanks are popular with hikers. Since the rock is broken and decomposing, extreme caution must be exercised when climbing this spire. Routes appear easy, but some of the rock is poor, which makes it difficult to place good protection.

To reach the spire from Kain Hut or Applebee Dome, follow the Cobalt Lake Trail as marked by the B.C. Ministry of Parks map. Route-finding skills are necessary since several mountain passes, small glaciers, and snowfields must be crossed to gain access to its flanks. The Blue Lake Trail near Hans Gmoser's CMH Heli-lodge may be another alternative to approaching Cobalt Lake. This route climbs through an old burn (forest fire) to Blue Lake and then cuts through high alpine meadows toward Cobalt Lake.

Route Descriptions

A   North Ridge

II

Approach: From Kain Hut or Applebee Dome, same as for Cobalt Lake. Gain W Ridge at saddle near Brenta Spire's S Ridge. Scramble ridge to steep 300-foot headwall. Ascend to left, three pitches, to upper N Ridge. Scramble to summit. **Time:** 3 hours from Kain Hut. **Descent:** Down-climb same route.

B   Southwest Face

II

Approach: Same as for N Ridge. Traverse below W Ridge to where a large rotten couloir can be ascended to summit. Early in season, couloir may contain snow. In late summer, plan for rotten scree and talus. Details unavailable.

BRENTA SPIRE
9650 ft. (2942 m)

Appearance and Location

Brenta Spire dominates the cirque above Cobalt Lake. It is part of a ridge that extends north to Northpost Spire and south and east to connect indirectly with Cobalt Lake Spire. Although it is the highest of this group, it is not visible from the Crescent Glacier, which is surrounded by Snowpatch, Bugaboo, Crescent, and Eastpost spires. Brenta's summit block is the only feature that resembles a spire, which bisects the north-south ridges that extend from it.

The blocky E Face drops steeply to snowfields above Cobalt Lake. The W Face is expansive and extends toward the Vowell Glacier. The sharp N Ridge extends directly to Northpost Spire. The S Ridge descends toward the eastern end of the north slopes of the Crescent Towers.

Notable First Ascent

A large party of five scrambled Brenta's easy S Ridge to its unexplored summit during the summer of 1938. L. Coveney, S. B. Hendricks, P. Olton, P. Prescott, and M. Schnellbacher approached the peak via the now popular Cobalt Lake Trail from Kain Hut. Once over the Eastpost-Crescent Saddle, they gained a col on the S Ridge that extends to the Crescent Towers and the Brenta-Crescent Col. From this point, it was an easy (albeit long) scramble to the summit blocks.

Climbing Brenta Spire

No technical climbing routes exist on this spire to date. However, the E Face offers several hundred feet of steep, exposed granite. Brenta is comprised of better quality rock than Cobalt Lake Spire. The popular S Ridge Route is an excellent scramble with great views of Bugaboo Spire, the Vowell Glacier and Vowell Group, and Cobalt Lake. A first visit to the Bugaboos can often be an intimidating experience to many crag climbers. A route like the S Ridge of Brenta Spire is a good warm-up for the long and committing routes on some of the other spires.

Access to Brenta is relatively easy. Follow the Cobalt Lake Trail from Kain Hut or Applebee Dome, through the Eastpost-Crescent Saddle to the Brenta-Crescent Col.

Route Descriptions

A   South Ridge

II

Approach: Hike Cobalt Lake Trail through Eastpost-Crescent Saddle to Brenta-Crescent Col. Scramble ridge to summit. **Time:** 2–3 hours from Kain Hut. **Descent:** Down-climb same route.

B   North Ridge

II

Approach: Same as for Northpost Spire. Although the first ascent party traversed N Ridge from Northpost Spire, it is not a popular route because of logistics. One of the best access routes for Northpost's summit is via Brenta's S Ridge, then reverse first ascent party's route and traverse the N Ridge to Northpost.

NORTHPOST SPIRE
9550 ft. (2910 m)

Appearance and Location

Northpost, part of the Cobalt Lake Cirque, is the farthest north of all the Bugaboo Group. Its summit is the culmination of three distinct ridges. Thus, three major faces offer technical climbing challenges.

The SW Ridge extends to meet Brenta Spire. The long, broken, and blocky face that drops west to the Vowell Glacier is over 1500 feet high. The east side is steeper, but it is half the height and holds a large snowfield that is poised above Cobalt Lake.

The broken E Ridge descends steeply to the outlet of Cobalt Lake. Its northeast face drops abruptly to a snowfield in the small basin below. From the northern shore of Cobalt Lake, the slightly less steep, southeastern slopes of this ridge rise to the summit.

The N Ridge, with much exposed rock on both its east and west flanks, descends from the summit toward the Vowell Creek basin. The west slopes of this ridge drop nearly 2000 feet to the Vowell Glacier, and the east side is equally exposed but half the height.

Notable First Ascents

Northpost's summit was first visited during the summer of 1938 by D. P. and I. A. Richards. They established a base camp near the tongue of the Vowell Glacier, from which they scrambled the N Ridge. They finished their climb on easy rock slightly to the northeast of the ridge proper.

Fred Beckey and Gerry Fuller pioneered the first technical route when they ascended the 2000-foot NW Face in August 1966. Although the climb was only moderate Class 5, it has seen few subsequent ascents.

Climbing Northpost Spire

Since Northpost is best approached from either Cobalt Lake or the Vowell Glacier, it is seldom visited. More often than not, climbers descend from Brenta and traverse the connecting ridge to Northpost. This can be a long day, but two nice summits can be bagged easily this way. The rock quality does not compare to that of the larger Bugaboo peaks, but it offers sound protection placement.

To approach Northpost's western flanks, cross the Bugaboo-Crescent Col and descend the Vowell Glacier. In doing this, be aware of loose rock in the col and crevasse danger on the Vowell Glacier. For climbs on Northpost's eastern and northeastern flanks, approach via the Cobalt Lake Trail from Kain Hut as marked on the B.C. Ministry of Parks map. Another feasible route is the Blue Lake Trail from Hans Gmoser's CMH Heli-lodge. See the park map (fig. 1) for access details.

Route Descriptions

A   North Ridge/Northeast Rocks

II

Approach: From Kain Hut, via Bugaboo-Crescent Col and Vowell Glacier to base of ridge. Scramble ridge, following line of least resistance to summit blocks. Traverse to the northeast and scramble easy rocks to summit. *Time:* 2 hours from basecamp near Vowell Glacier. *Descent:* Down-climb same route.

B   Northwest Face

III   5.6–5.7

Approach: Same as for N Ridge. Follow slabby depression in the face, which is east of central buttress. Climb buttress directly. No details of technical pitches available from vague account— moderately difficult climbing on rock that is of lesser quality than of central Bugaboos. *Time:* 4–6 hours from Vowell Glacier. *Descent:* Down-climb N Ridge.

C   Northwest Face-West Side

III   5.5–5.6

Approach: Same as for N Ridge. Route is several hundred feet right of regular NW Face Route. Climb face right of slabs to steep headwall (easy Class 5). Climb up several hundred feet to a ledge (5.3–5.4). Final 600 feet of route follows a dihedral to summit (5.5–5.6). *Time:* 4–6 hours from Vowell Glacier. *Descent:* Down-climb N Ridge.

CRESCENT SPIRE
9350 ft. (2843 m)

Appearance and Location

Although the rounded summit of Crescent Spire is the highest point of the cirque that forms the northern boundary of the Crescent Glacier, it bears little resemblance to a spire. Crescent Spire

Climbers discuss routes on Snowpatch Spire; Pigeon Spire in the background.

is slightly northwest of the Crescent Towers' three distinct summits along this obvious east-west ridge-line. The two prominent dihedral formations that cleave Crescent Spire's steep S Face, called the McTech Arete Area, distinguish it from the neighboring Crescent Towers.

A northeastern ridge extends from Crescent Spire's summit toward Cobalt Lake, which merges with Brenta Spire's S Ridge at the Crescent-Brenta Col. Its western ridge descends gently to join with Bugaboo Spire's NE Ridge at the Bugaboo-Crescent Col.

Notable First Ascents

Conrad Kain guided J. Monroe Thorington up the easy southeast slopes to gain Crescent Spire's untouched summit in June 1933.

The first technical routes were pioneered by Brian Greenwood and Richard Lofthouse during the summer of 1968, when they climbed the two prominent dihedrals that cleave the S Face. This steep 800-foot face has become the only true sport cragging area in the Bugaboos at present. The first free ascent of this face was done by Pat McNurtney and Doug Klewin 10 years later, in 1978, when they climbed the arete that separates the two large dihedrals and named it McTech Arete. Now most climbers know the S Face of Crescent Spire only by its nickname, the McTech Area.

Climbing Crescent Spire

Excluding the S Face, other features of the spire are easily attained by scrambling. The S Face, however, is of particular interest to the modern technical climber. Over a dozen quality crack routes exist in the McTech Area alone. The rock on Crescent varies in quality. Some of the orange-yellow colored granite is dirty, granular, and decomposing. Other spots on the spire are covered with black lichen, although some of the hard, white rock is clean and sharply fractured. Many flakes and edges are razor sharp and can damage mismanaged ropes. Some flaring and many parallel cracks exist, warranting the use of camming devices for good protection. A modern standard rack of Friends, nuts, RPs, and TCUs is recommended.

Very few fixed points of protection, belay, or rappel stations exist. In addition, although most climbers do not use helmets, rockfall danger exists, and ledges are often strewn with loose rocks. Although popular, and only an hour hike from Kain Hut, this area does not get the traffic that a more accessible roadside crag might, so use discretion when climbing here.

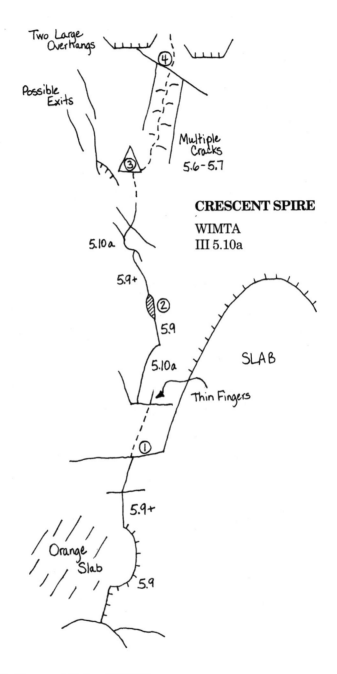

Fig. 5. *Crescent Spire, WIMTA*

The standard approach from Kain Hut is no more than a strenuous one-hour hike up the moraine trail above the hut via Applebee Dome. Once past Applebee, skirt the tarns and gain the upper Crescent Glacier. From the neve, it is a casual walk to the base of the obvious dihedral formations. Only minor crevasse danger exists on the upper Crescent Glacier, but caution is advised for any glacier approaches.

Descents are numerous and generally involve easy down-climbing through scree gullies. However, a descent to Bugaboo-Crescent Col offers multiple rappel points and avoids the sharp scree of the SW Gully.

Route Descriptions

AA Southeast Slopes

Class 4

Approach: Via the Eastpost-Crescent Saddle. Scramble on rock and snow up easy slopes to summit block. *Time:* 1–2 hours from Kain Hut. *Descent:* Down-climb same route.

BB Southwest Gully

Class 4

Approach: Via upper Crescent Glacier. Scramble easy sandy, scree-filled gully to notch between highest Crescent Tower and main peak. This is one of the standard descents. *Time:* 1–2 hours from Kain Hut. *Descent:* Down-climb same route.

CC West Ridge

5.2–5.3

Approach: Via upper Crescent Glacier. **1–2** Climb Bugaboo-Crescent Col to ridge crest (easy Class **4–5**; beware of rockfall danger). Scramble easy ground up blocky ridge to main summit. *Time:* 2–3 hours from Kain Hut. *Descent:* Down-climb and rappel same route or down-climb SW Gully.

DD WIMTA (Who Is McTech Anyway?)

III 5.10b *(fig. 5)*

Approach: Via upper Crescent Glacier. Start 500 feet left of the left dihedral on the S Face. **1–3** Climb difficult cracks left of large slab capped by an arch. **4–5** Move right and follow easier cracks through two large roofs to ridge crest (possible direct finish above pitch 3). *Time:* 3 hours from base. *Descent:* Down-climb and rappel W Ridge.

Author Randall Green climbs the second pitch of Energy Crisis.

A   Paddle Flake/Left Dihedral Variation

III   5.10b *(fig. 6) (photo, p. 42)*

Approach: Via upper Crescent Glacier. At the base of the left-most prominent dihedral, several large blocks are stacked against the left wall. **1** Climb left side of blocks to ledge. **2–3** Follow main dihedral, first moving right above loose stacked flakes to ramp on right wall, then back left to ledge. Follow main dihedral to alcove and face-climb left. **4–6** Jam right side (finger-size crack, crux) of large detached flake, shaped like a paddle. From top of flake, climb arching hand cracks up through roof to easier cracks that lead to the exit chimney. Tricky in spots, but generally a good climb with well-protected sustained sections. **Time:** 4–6 hours from base. **Descent:** Down-climb and rappel W Ridge.

B   South Face-Left Dihedral

III   5.8/A2 *(fig. 6) (photo, p. 42)*

Approach: Via upper Crescent Glacier. Follow general line of main left dihedral. **1–2** Climb first two pitches of Paddle Flake Variation. **3–5** Aid through small roof, above the alcove, move right to easier cracks; follow right wall until it is possible to exit on W Ridge. **Time:** 4–6 hours from base. **Descent:** Down-climb and rappel W Ridge.

C   Roof McTech

5.10 *(fig. 6) (photo, p. 42)*

Approach: Via upper Crescent Glacier. Direct start to McTech Arete that is the next major crack system left of the overhanging arching dihedral called Energy Crisis. This strenuous, two-pitch hand crack splits a prominent roof that extends from the middle of the right wall of the left dihedral to the broken arete formation that separates the two main dihedral formations. Continue up McTech Arete to top. **Time:** 4–6 hours from base. **Descent:** Down-climb and rappel W Ridge or down-climb SW Gully.

D   Energy Crisis

5.11c *(fig. 6) (photo, p. 42)*

Approach: Via upper Crescent Glacier. Direct start to McTech Arete, which follows a striking open book formation that arches up and slightly left. This classic two-pitch formation combines delicate stemming with strenuous liebacking and technical jamming—an excellent climb with two semi-hanging belays. Take protection for parallel, thin, finger-size cracks that widen to

McTech Arete Area, Crescent Spire, S Face

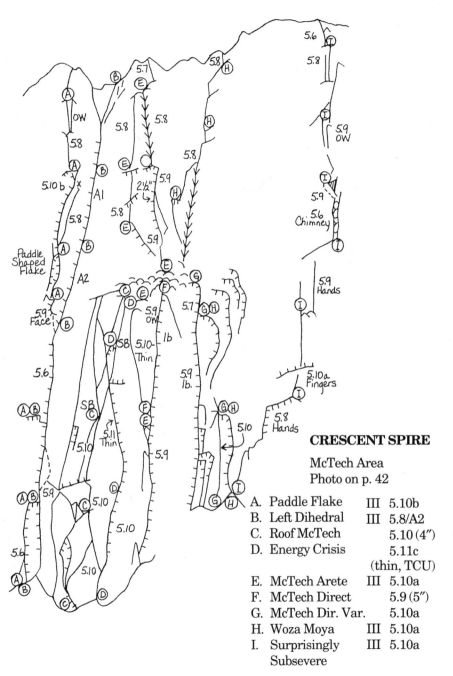

CRESCENT SPIRE

McTech Area
Photo on p. 42

A.	Paddle Flake	III	5.10b
B.	Left Dihedral	III	5.8/A2
C.	Roof McTech		5.10 (4″)
D.	Energy Crisis		5.11c (thin, TCU)
E.	McTech Arete	III	5.10a
F.	McTech Direct		5.9 (5″)
G.	McTech Dir. Var.		5.10a
H.	Woza Moya	III	5.10a
I.	Surprisingly Subsevere	III	5.10a

Fig. 6. Crescent Spire, McTech Area

3-inch flared cracks near top. Continue up McTech Arete to top. *Time:* 4–6 hours from base. *Descent:* Down-climb and rappel W Ridge or down-climb SW Gully.

E McTech Arete

III 5.10a *(fig. 6) (photo, p. 42)*

Approach: Via upper Crescent Glacier. This popular route follows three minor open book formations that are obvious breaks on the arete, separating the two prominent dihedrals on the S Face. **1** Climb first open book formation right of Energy Crisis, good hand crack. **2** Continue up book 15 feet until it is possible to climb hand/finger crack on left wall of open book, avoiding offwidth above. **3–6** Climb hand cracks past small roofs and spacious ledges to easier ground and summit. An excellent climb that can be protected with a standard rack. *Time:* 4–6 hours from base. *Descent:* Down-climb and rappel W Ridge or down-climb SW Gully.

F McTech Direct

5.9 *(fig. 6) (photo, p. 42)*

Approach: This one-pitch variation ascends the first pitch of McTech Arete and then continues up the open book formation and directly attacks the offwidth above. Lieback with strenuous fist jams around chockstone near the top of the offwidth. Continue on McTech Arete to top. *Time:* 4–6 hours from base. *Descent:* Same as for McTech Arete.

G McTech Direct-Variation Right

5.10a *(fig. 6) (photo, p. 42)*

Approach: About 20 feet right of the main McTech open book are a group of flakes that appear to be stacked vertically against the left wall of the right dihedral. This three-pitch variation ascends clean, sharp cracks formed by the flake edges up the left wall to the block terrace of the midpoint of McTech Arete; excellent cracks and good protection with nuts and Friends. Continue up McTech Arete to top. *Time:* 4–6 hours from base. *Descent:* Same as for McTech Arete.

H Woza Moya/Right Dihedral

III 5.6/A2 or 5.10a *(fig. 6) (photo, p. 42)*

Approach: Same as for McTech Arete. This route more or less ascends the right-most dihedral formation on the S Face. **1–2** Follow jam cracks up main corner to broken Class 4 area. **3–6** Climb straight up corner, easy Class 5 to nice ledge on left wall. Continue up crack on left wall and friction right into main corner system to finish. Good climb on good rock, standard protection rack. *Time:* 4–6 hours from base. **Descent:** Down-climb SW Gully.

I   Surprisingly Subsevere

III 5.10a *(fig. 6) (photo, p. 42)*

Approach: Same as for McTech Arete. Start 20 feet right of right dihedral and follow cracks up right wall. **1** Climb flake and cracks, constantly moving right at breaks, belay below roof. **2–3** Climb through roof, follow cracks right to another ramp below a large overhang. Move right on ramp, belay at blocks in chimney. **4–6** Climb chimney, offwidth, and cracks to summit. Route meanders through rock that is often covered in black lichen, protection good with standard rack. *Time:* 4–6 hours from base. *Descent:* Down-climb SW Gully.

J   Northeast Ridge

Class 4

Approach: Via Eastpost-Crescent Saddle/Crescent-Brenta Col. This scramble route is most often used when traversing Crescent and Brenta spires. *Time:* 2 hours from Kain Hut. **Descent:** Down-climb same route.

CRESCENT TOWERS
9000 ft. (2737 m)

Appearance and Location

The Crescent Towers dominate the Crescent Group, not in stature but in appearance. These towers beckon the rock climber, but close inspection reveals their lower slopes to be covered with moss and rubble. The upper, steep rock faces are split with abundant cracks, but many are covered in thick black lichen. The four distinct summits all present climbing challenges, however, and several good climbing routes exist on their steep southern faces.

The S Tower, known as the Donkey's Ears, is the best known of the group. The twin summit is split by a large chimney on the southwestern face, which adds to the earlike appearance. The SE Ridge of the eastern ear merges with Eastpost Spire at the

View of the Crescent Group/Brenta Spire/Cobalt Lake Spire

Eastpost-Crescent Saddle. The western ear is part of the ridge that joins the other two towers.

The broken Central Tower is separated from the Donkey's Ears by a steep scree gully. Rising from the scree, steep ramps and blocky ridges predominate the Central Tower's lower, southern flanks. A ridge that extends to the northwest connects the Central Tower to the N Tower, which is highest in the group.

The N Tower stands alone like a castle turret. When viewed from the Crescent Glacier, it looks like a chess rook with a large steep slab, characterized by light brown-yellow rock, protecting the flat summit platform. The N Tower is separated from Crescent Spire by the SW Gully, steep and scree-filled, with very loose rock of all sizes.

Notable First Ascents

The N Tower was first ascended by Eaton Cromwell and G. Englehard in August 1938. They scrambled up the SW Gully to the N Ridge, from which they climbed easy, steep, and blocky ground to the summit.

Richard Lofthouse first led a CMC party to the Donkey's Ears in 1968. Lofthouse pioneered a technical route up the dihedral and chimney that splits the ears.

CMH (heli-skiing) founder Hans Gmoser guided Mr. and Mrs. T. Hindset up the first technical route of the Central Tower in 1969.

Climbing Crescent Towers

Only the S and W faces are of much interest to technical climbers. Many scramble routes are possible on their eastern slopes. The rock is generally sound, although lighter in color and softer than much of the rest of the Bugaboo batholith. Wind erosion and the acidic secretions from the black lichen that inhabit most of the Crescent Towers has contributed to the rock's very rough, abrasive texture.

Countless unclimbed crack systems abound, especially on the S Tower, but often first ascent parties encounter dirt in the cracks and lichen so thick it is like fur. However, after successive ascents of a line, or some cleaning, the routes are very enjoyable and vary in degrees of difficulty and commitment.

Many of the lower slopes of all the towers are low-angle with sloping ledges strewn with loose rock. Helmets are recommended on all routes and rockfall danger is always present. Climbing the aretes, ridges, or steep faces is always safer than the many scree gullies. A rack of standard protection hardware is adequate for most routes (see figs. 7–9 for details).

Approaches are relatively quick and easy from Kain Hut or Applebee Dome. All glacier travel can be avoided if necessary by scrambling along moraine ridges along the east side of the Crescent Glacier. Descents are generally easy down-climbs off the north and east sides of the towers to gain access to either the SW Gully between Crescent Spire and the N Tower or by scrambling down the SE Ridge toward Eastpost Spire.

Route Descriptions

NORTH TOWER

A   North Ridge

Class 4

Approach: From southeast, via Crescent Glacier moraine slopes above Applebee Dome to SW Gully. Ascend SW Gully between Crescent Spire and the N Tower. At ridge crest, scramble broken rock along prominent N Ridge to summit. *Time:* 2 hours from Kain Hut. *Descent:* Down-climb same route.

B   Northwest Ridge—Southwest Gully Right

II   5.4

Approach: Same as for N Ridge. Climb a minor ridge or arete that forms the right side of the SW Gully; ridge leads directly to summit. **1–3** Follow crest up moderately difficult rock, some 5.4. **4–5** Ascend a narrow chimney, 5.2–5.3 (300 feet) to final steep section. Scramble broken rock to summit. *Time:* 2–3 hours from SW Gully. *Descent:* Down-climb N Ridge.

CENTRAL TOWERS

C   Northwest Gully

Class 4 *(photo, p. 49)*

Approach: Same as for NW Ridge-SW Gully Right. Between the N and Central towers are a series of gullies and ramps. Scramble the easiest gully and follow the line of least resistance (Class 4). *Time:* 1.5 hours from Kain Hut. *Descent:* Down-climb same route.

D   Lion's Way

II   5.6 *(fig. 7) (photo, p. 49)*

Approach: From southeast, via Crescent Glacier moraine slopes above Applebee Dome to base of buttress. This popular route follows the W Buttress. Good route-finding skills may be helpful;

Crescent Spire/McTech Arete Area/Crescent Towers

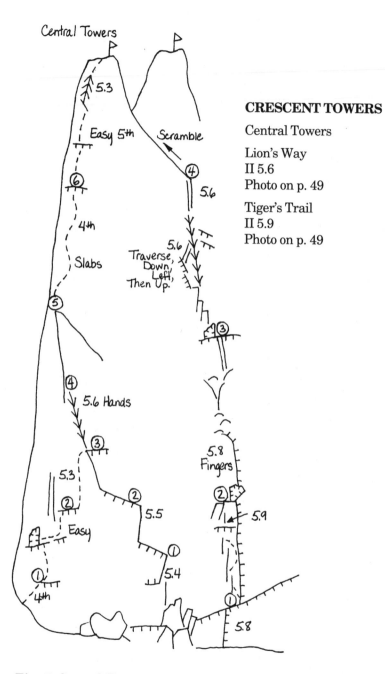

Central Towers

5.3

Easy 5th

Scramble

6

4th

Slabs

5

4

5.6 Hands

3

5.3

2

Easy

1

4th

2

5.5

1

5.4

CRESCENT TOWERS

Central Towers

Lion's Way
II 5.6
Photo on p. 49

Tiger's Trail
II 5.9
Photo on p. 49

4

5.6

5.6

Traverse,
Down,
Then Up.
Left,

3

5.8
Fingers

2

5.9

1

5.8

Fig. 7. *Central Towers, Lion's Way and Tiger's Trail*

follow worn trail up lichen-covered rock. **1–3** Climb flakes and ledge systems to gain the proper W Buttress. **4–5** Ascend inside corner (crux) and cracks to natural break in buttress. **6–7** Scramble easy ground to section of short, steep steps (easy Class 5). **8** Climb low-angle inside corner to summit. **Time:** 3–4 hours from base. **Descent:** Down-climb NW Gully or E Face and cross Eastpost-Crescent Saddle.

E   Tiger's Trail

II   5.9 *(fig. 7) (photo, p. 49)*

Approach: Same as for Lion's Way. This route ascends a more direct line to the notch between the two Central Tower summits. **1–2** Climb a strenuous flake to a grassy ledge and then climb cracks to a belay. **3–4** Continue to climb straight up via flakes and cracks to another ledge. Move left and climb over and down flakes to gain another crack system. Scramble to notch. **Time:** 3–4 hours from base. **Descent:** Same as for Lion's Way.

SOUTH TOWER DONKEY'S EARS

F   Thatcher Cracker

III   5.10 *(fig. 8) (photo, p. 49)*

Approach: Same as for Lion's Way. A committed line, this route follows the west side of the S Face of the western ear (see topo). **1–2** Climb a shallow inside corner and crack left of a large roof to grassy ledge. Then follow easy flakes to belay below crescent-shaped flakes. **3–5** Easy liebacks lead to 5.9 + hand crack, which ends at a small ledge. Continue to follow flakes and cracks through blocky area and more good cracks. **6** Climb an inside stemming corner to north shoulder below summit (5.10, no protection). **Time:** 4–5 hours from base. **Descent:** Same as for Tiger's Trail or by traversing eastern slopes toward SE Ridge and the Eastpost-Crescent Saddle.

G   Ears Between

II   5.7 *(fig. 9) (photo, p. 49)*

Approach: Same as for Lion's Way. Originally pioneered by Lofthouse, the route's start has many variations, but the more popular ones are from the large grassy ledge that angles up from the lower west side of the S Face. **1–3** From the grassy ledge climb flakes and blocks. **4–5** Move left and mantle onto a large ramp. Work up cracks and flakes to gain main chimney, belay in alcove. **6** Chimney to notch between the ears. **Time:** 4 hours from base. **Descent:** Traverse the east slopes to gain the SE Ridge.

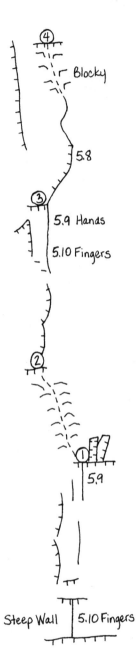

CRESCENT TOWERS

Donkey's Ears

Thatcher Cracker
III 5.10
Photo on p. 49
Protection:
    2 sets Friends to #4
    Extra to 6"
    1 set TCUs to #2
    1 set wires

Fig. 8. *Crescent Towers, Thatcher Cracker*

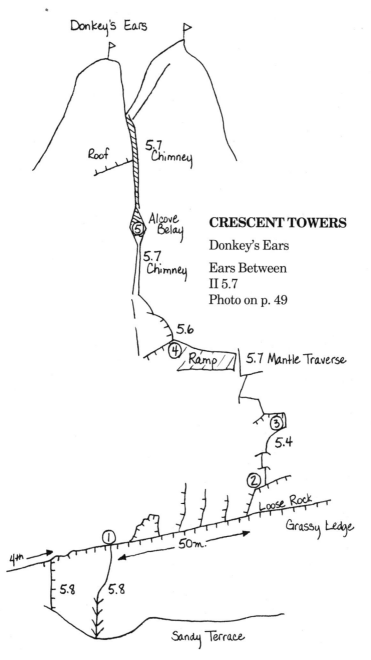

Fig. 9. *Crescent Towers, Ears Between*

BUGABOO SPIRE
10,450 ft. (3176 m)

Appearance and Location

From the moraine and snowfields above Kain Hut or from the tenting sites at Applebee Dome, the massive twin spires of Snowpatch and Bugaboo tower over the landscape. Slightly higher than Snowpatch, Bugaboo looms above the northern end of the Crescent Glacier.

Viewed from the east, the dramatic profiles of the S and NE ridges (both extremely popular climbing routes) are revealed. Seen from the west, it becomes immediately clear why the W Face of Bugaboo is almost never climbed. The base of this face is protected by the very broken eastern edge of the Vowell Glacier. The face itself is a complex mosaic of ledge systems, dihedrals, and flake systems.

Perhaps the most attractive views of Bugaboo are from the north and northwest—views seldom seen by Bugaboo visitors. From the lower Vowell Glacier (formerly called the Warren Glacier) the northern aspects of Bugaboo are truly spirelike.

Bugaboo has two distinct summits. The S Summit, slightly lower of the two, is the summit reached via the standard S Ridge (Kain) Route. The true summit is another half-hour scramble to the north.

Notable First Ascents

Of all his noteworthy climbs, Conrad Kain referred to his 1916 ascent of Bugaboo Spire's S Ridge as his most difficult. Indeed, the gendarme pitch near the summit of Bugaboo was an incredibly ambitious undertaking for the time: 5.5–5.6 climbing, with tremendous exposure on an unclimbed peak. For Kain and his friends, Albert and Bess MacCarthy and John Vincent, it must have been an extraordinary feeling to have knocked off perhaps the most difficult rock climb yet accomplished in North America.

So sheer and intimidating was Bugaboo that it took 42 years for a second route to be finished on the spire. In 1958, Dave Croft, John Turner, Richard Sykes, and David Isles climbed the elegant NE Ridge and a real Bugaboo classic was established. The following two years saw a flurry of activity as modern aid and free climbing techniques by such notables as Fred Beckey, Ed Cooper, and Layton Kor led to ascents of the E, W, and N faces.

Crescent Spire/McTech Arete Area/Crescent Towers,
as seen from Bugaboo Spire S Ridge (note the two
climbers on Bugaboo Spire E Face)

Climbing Bugaboo Spire

The amazing thing about climbing on Bugaboo Spire is that so *few* routes have been established on this tremendous piece of granite, and that only two of these routes see any real activity. Novice climbers and Bugaboo newcomers of all abilities scamper happily up the Kain Route, and on fair mornings there is sometimes a line to get on the classic NE Ridge.

Without a doubt, these two routes deserve their popularity. The Kain Route is a low-commitment scramble, with just two short bits of 5.5–5.6 climbing—the ideal opportunity for getting up high on a spire without difficult climbing. The NE Ridge is in the Roper-Steck book, *Fifty Classic Climbs in North America,* and about halfway up the fourth pitch you will understand why. The route offers five pitches of pleasant, moderate climbing, and then the *real* fun begins: sensational alpine Class 4 ridge travel, with tremendous drops off each side of the narrow ridge, and truly spectacular views.

Other than these two standards, very little is done on Bugaboo Spire—the normal E Face (Cooper/Gran) Route sees one or two ascents each season; the other established routes are virtually never climbed.

This is partly due to access. While it is easy to reach the E Face of Bugaboo (and the adjacent S and NE ridges) from Kain Hut, approaching the N and W faces requires considerably more effort. Approaches for all climbs on Bugaboo generally begin with the slog up the moraine above Kain Hut, to reach the upper Crescent Glacier (this makes the tenting sites at Applebee Dome very convenient, especially for routes on the E Face).

Perhaps the most difficult (and most dangerous) aspect of climbing the Kain Ridge is the ascent to the Bugaboo-Snowpatch Col. Negotiating the bergschrund can sometimes be tricky, depending on the season. Ice axes and mountain boots are necessary, and parties should consider roping for this approach at the base of the couloir. Watch for rockfall, and be especially wary of the right side of the couloir, beneath the very loose eastern flank of the S Ridge. These precautions are particularly important during late-afternoon descents of this couloir.

Similarly, the worst objective hazards of the NE Ridge route might be encountered on the scramble from the head of the Crescent Glacier to the Bugaboo-Crescent Col. This is a half-hour Class 3 to Class 4 scramble on generally sound rock, but there is danger from stonefall and fair exposure. Belaying this approach is slow, but it may be advisable for climbers with little mountain experience. Remember those below you and *be careful of loose rock!*

Author Joe Bensen leads an airy Bugaboo pitch.

Climbers ascend the Bugaboo-Snowpatch Col; Pigeon Spire in the background.

Once these initial obstacles are overcome, both standard routes on Bugaboo generally are safe and highly enjoyable. But keep in mind that both routes are full-day excursions, and an eye to the weather is necessary. Bugaboo is the chief lightning rod in the area, and even these easy routes can turn quickly into hair-raising epics. We advise predawn starts from Kain Hut for either route, in order to be off the mountain before the common late-afternoon weather change.

The rest of Bugaboo is wide open and rarely climbed. There are four routes on the sheer E Face, two on the W, and two on the N. The W Face rock is said to be of poorer quality, but the N and E faces are considered sound. There is tremendous potential for pioneering new routes on Bugaboo, especially on the N and NW faces.

The recommended descent from the summit of Bugaboo is via the Kain Route, which is mostly a walk-off with a few easy rappels (single rope will do). The first rappel is directly off the S Summit. A word of caution regarding the second rappel (from the gendarme) is in order. Do *not* attempt to rap down the west side of the gendarme, even though this may seem the likely line of descent from the well-established station above the gendarme. Doing so will require a long pendulum to gain the easy ridge-line; failing to make this swing (due, for instance, to poor visibility) will send you unhappily down the W Face.

The proper rappel is down the back (E) side of the gendarme. Scramble up and left 50 feet (west, behind a prominent flake) to a chockstone, and the third rappel station. Two more short, traversing rappels are followed by an airy scramble along a knife-edged ridge, about 100 feet to a flat spot. The rappel is off the south end of this tower. There is some moderate down-climbing below this point (some parts of which might require the rope), and one more rappel is possible to avoid down-climbing a steep chimney.

Then it is just a long (somewhat tedious) walk-off, finishing at the Bugaboo-Snowpatch Col. Stay close to the ridge crest, generally as far to the west as possible, and avoid the temptation to descend the gullies that drop onto the E Face. Climbs of the NE Ridge and most of the E and N face routes finish at the N Summit. The traverse of this summit ridge is one of the real highlights of climbing in the Bugaboos, and we recommend it highly.

The following summit shortcut is meant to facilitate getting off Bugaboo quickly in bad weather, or when pressed for time. In bad weather, the N and S summit blocks can be avoided by a series of short rappels and traverses, generally on the upper E Face. From the east side of the N Summit block, rappel 50 feet to a ledge system. Regain the saddle between the two summits by traversing several hundred feet south. Follow the knife-edged ridge to the

Bugaboo Spire, S Ridge

lowest point of the saddle, at a prominent 45-degree slab above the W Face (may be wet); traverse this slab 100 feet to a wall below the S Summit block. Angle up and left (southeast) to the obvious notch (rappel station). Rappel 50 feet into a low-angled gully, then traverse west to the pedestal just above the gendarme and a final short rappel onto the upper Kain Route. At this point you are at the rappel station above the gendarme.

Route Descriptions

A   South Ridge/Kain Route

III   5.5–5.6 *(fig. 10) (photo, p. 60)*

Approach: Via Crescent Glacier and Bugaboo-Snowpatch Col (1–2 hours from Boulder Camp). Route follows line of least resistance along ridge crest to S Summit. Ascend a right-sloping ramp above the bivouac area to gain broken slopes that lead to ridge crest at mid-height (Class 3). Scramble two steep chimneys that split short steps on upper ridge (Class 4). **1–4** From top flat pedestal on ridge crest below south side of gendarme, climb broken southern edge to comfortable belay block; ascend ramp to right and climb past fixed pins in diagonal cracks on steep S Wall of gendarme, then friction across slabby west side of gendarme to large flat ledge. Climb a few pitches of Class 4 and easy Class 5 up gully on left side of summit block to top of S Summit. Several more challenging variations are possible to surmount the gendarme (see topo). *Time:* 5–6 hours from Kain Hut. *Descent:* Rappel and down-climb same route, allow 2 hours for descent. (Details of rappels are described in Climbing Bugaboo Spire section, p. 56. Rap stations are also marked on fig. 10.)

WEST FACE

(photo, p. 60)

Approach: Via the Crescent Glacier and Bugaboo-Snowpatch Col to Vowell Glacier (1–2 hours from Kain Hut). Avoid icefall by descending from upper Vowell to main glacier several hundred feet west of Bugaboo's W Face. Below icefall, move east to regain foot of face. Beware of potential crevasse danger on all glaciers.

B   West Face

IV   5.4 *(fig. 10) (photos, pp. 60, 63)*

This route ascends a series of ramps and ledge systems in a zigzag toward the S Summit. From a talus cone on the lower middle of the face, scramble broken rock to left-sloping ramp, traverse to top of a lower black headwall. **1–4** Traverse left to ledge system

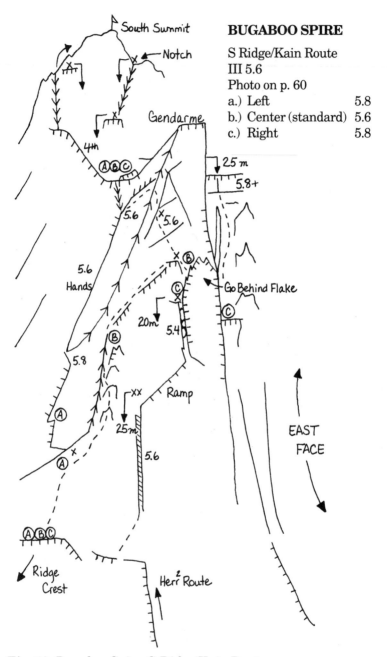

BUGABOO SPIRE

S Ridge/Kain Route
III 5.6
Photo on p. 60
a.) Left   5.8
b.) Center (standard) 5.6
c.) Right   5.8

Fig. 10. Bugaboo Spire, S Ridge/Kain Route
Photo: *Bugaboo Spire, NW Face*

that works through another ramp and slab section. **5–7** Ascend a vertical jam crack to gain ramp that angles up and to right of huge, rotten, white wall above. **8–10** Follow shallow, slabby trough to foot of steep wall (approximately 300 feet) directly below summit. **11–13** Lieback and chimney steep flakes to final strenuous, but easy (5.4) pitch to thin ridge crest. Class 4 along ridge to S Summit. Numerous variations are possible on this complex face (approximately 2000 feet of rock climbing). *Time:* 9–10 hours from Kain Hut. *Descent:* Same as for Kain Route.

C   West Face Direct

IV   5.4/A2 *(fig. 10) (photos, pp. 63, 65)*

Essentially the same route as described above with exceptions as follows: from left-sloping ramp, ascend steep wall and chimney (aid used to pass overhang in chimney); from top of slabby trough, work up diagonally right to gain Kain Route below gendarme. Follow Kain Route to S Summit. *Time:* 9–10 hours from Kain Hut. *Descent:* Same as for Kain Route.

NORTH FACE

(photo, p. 65)

Approach: Same as for W Face or via Bugaboo-Crescent Col to low-angled snow slopes above the Vowell Glacier.

D   North Face

IV   5.7/A1 *(photos, pp. 63, 65)*

An inverted "U" or square-shaped slot characterizes the lower portion of the face; this route ascends a line left (Kruszyna-Putnam guide suggests route is to right of slot) of the slot and follows left-slanting diagonal cracks on the upper wall to N Summit. Climb Class 4 and easy Class 5 up a black dike gully to pedestal/flake ledge. Traverse ledge left and climb flakes and cracks several pitches to gain long ledge system. Move right to end of ledge and follow large left-slanting open book up steep wall to less steep ground. Work right to base of white N Summit block and follow dihedral system up middle left side of white wall. Details of this serious 2000-foot route are unclear (see marked photo, p. 00). In addition to a standard rack, knifeblade and Lost Arrow pitons may be necessary. *Time:* 9 hours from base. *Descent:* Same as for Kain Route. (See description for descent from N Summit in Climbing Bugaboo Spire section, p. 56.)

Bugaboo Spire, N Face

Bugaboo Spire, NE Ridge

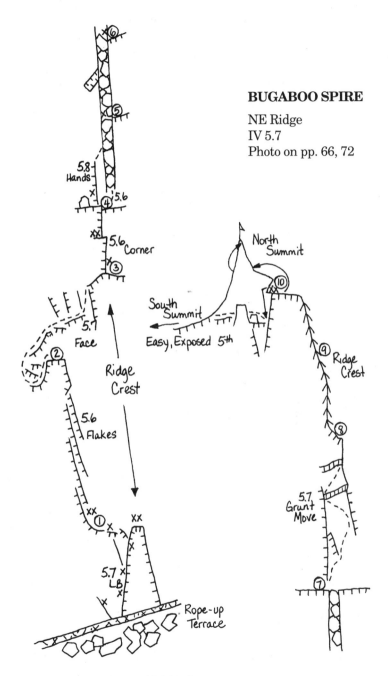

BUGABOO SPIRE

NE Ridge
IV 5.7
Photo on pp. 66, 72

Fig. 11. Bugaboo Spire, NE Ridge

E   North Face Direct

IV   5.10/A1 *(photo, p. 65)*

The direct variant takes an independent line up the lower third of the face and joins the original N Face Route at the second major ledge system. Several hundred feet left (east) of original route, climb low-angled, large left-facing open books and flakes to gain second major ledge (8 pitches). Details unavailable. Continue on regular N Face Route to N Summit. *Time:* 9 hours from base. *Descent:* Same as for Kain Route.

F   Northeast Ridge

IV   5.7 *(fig. 11) (photos, pp. 66, 72)*

Approach: Ascend Crescent Glacier to head of cirque below lowest point of Bugaboo-Crescent Col. Scramble Class 3–4 right-sloping ramps, rubble-strewn ledges, and short steps to col. Walk west along ridge crest to slabs split by obvious wide crack system. Ascend easy cracks to intersection of white dike/ledge that girdles ridge and east side of E Face. **1–2** Lieback crack left of small pinnacle/flake 40 feet, then move right and stem/chimney left side of hollow detached flake. From top of flake, down-climb 6 feet, traverse left to flake system that angles toward E Face, and climb to small ledge at top of flakes. **3–6** Down-climb onto E Face until it is possible to double back (above belay), climbing flakes to white quartz dike and ridge crest. Belay from ledge at base of right-facing open book; climb dihedral (finger-size crack) to first major break in ridge. From this very large ledge, two distinct variations are possible in order to gain main chimney system of upper ridge. (1) Hand crack on left (straightforward but strenuous); (2) easier flakes and chimney with prominent rock spike, belay from atop large chockstone. Ascend easy Class 5 and Class 4 chimney to top of second break in ridge. Follow prominent corners and slabs to ridge crest and N Summit. Diverse climbing on excellent rock, comfortable belay stances, and breathtaking views contribute to the joys of climbing this route—unquestionably a classic. **Variation:** From top of pitch 1, traverse right to open book, which can be ascended (strenuous 5.7) to join normal route at top of pitch 3. *Time:* 7–8 hours from Kain Hut. *Descent:* Traverse summits and descend Kain Route.

G   Pretty Vacant

IV   5.9/A2 *(fig. 13) (photos, pp. 66, 72)*

Approach: Same as for NE Ridge. This route ascends a flake system from the quartz dike on right (east) edge of E Face and merges with NE Ridge (approximately pitch 7). Descend

Gene Klein scales the dihedral pitch of Bugaboo Spire, NE Ridge.

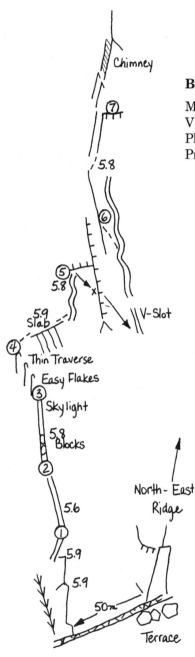

BUGABOO SPIRE

Midnight Route
V 5.9/A3
Photos on pp. 60, 72
Protection:
    2 sets Friends to #3$\frac{1}{2}$
    2 sets TCUs
    2 sets wires, extra RPs/HBs
    2 KB
    2 LA

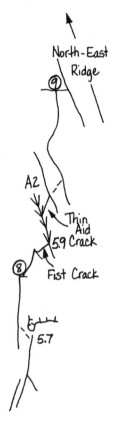

Fig. 12. Bugaboo Spire, Midnight Route

dike/terrace (150 feet left of NE Ridge start) toward the E Face. **1–4** Ascend flakes and chimneys to a series of steps formed by flakes. **5–7** From top of flake steps traverse right to gain parallel crack systems and V-slot that leads to ledge. **8–9** Climb diagonally toward the right continually moving to better cracks and NE Ridge Route to N Summit. *Time:* 9–10 hours from Kain Hut. *Descent:* Same as for NE Ridge.

EAST FACE

(photo, p. 72)

Approach by crossing the Crescent Glacier to the base of the E Face of Bugaboo (1 hour from Kain Hut).

H   Midnight Route

V   5.9/A3 *(fig. 12) (photos, pp. 60, 72)*

Approach: Same for all E Face routes (see E Face approach note above). Directly below the N Summit at the base of the wall, a large square-shaped block *used* to mark the beginning of this route and the normal E Face or Cooper-Gran Route. The back of the block formed a chimney that allowed easy access to the large crescent-shaped ledge ("the balcony") that cuts across the base of the E Face. Sometime during the winter of 1988–1989, the block disappeared. Several crack systems can be ascended to reach the "balcony," however.

1 Climb one long pitch of finger and hand cracks (5.10 or A1) to balcony. The Midnight Route follows a flake system that leads to the NE Ridge (see photos, pp. 00). **2–5** From balcony, aid short step to series of flakes that increase in angle and difficulty; two sling belays and difficult aid characterize these pitches. **6–8** Ascend flakes until it is possible to move right and face-climb to cracks that lead to big blocks/ledge. Move right on ledge and climb awkward flake to narrow ramp. **9–10** Climb flakes to roof, then go left to sling belay; work up and right along easy Class 5 to NE Ridge crest. First and second ascent parties finished last pitches in dark and bivied on good ledge at NE Ridge. Continue on NE Ridge to N Summit. *Time:* 1.5–2 days from base. *Descent:* Traverse summits and descend Kain Route.

I   East Face/Cooper-Gran Route

V   5.8/A2 or 5.11 *(fig. 14) (photos, pp. 60, 72)*

Approach: Same as for Midnight Route. This route lies farther left (south) and is parallel to the Midnight Route. **1** Climb first pitch of Midnight Route (see above). **2–3** Traverse balcony to W end (250 feet) and climb flake/groove system past black stain to

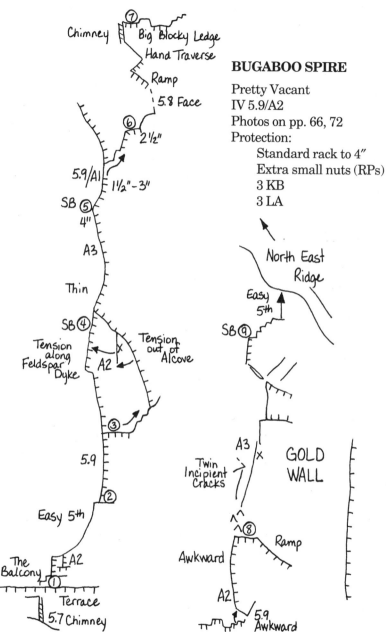

BUGABOO SPIRE

Pretty Vacant
IV 5.9/A2
Photos on pp. 66, 72
Protection:
    Standard rack to 4″
    Extra small nuts (RPs)
    3 KB
    3 LA

Fig. 13. *Bugaboo Spire, Pretty Vacant*
Photo: *Bugaboo Spire, E Face*

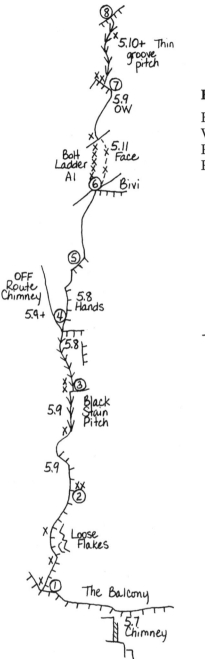

BUGABOO SPIRE

E Face/Cooper-Gran
V 5.9/A1 (5.11)
Photos on pp. 60, 72
Protection:
     2 sets Friends to #4
     TCUs to #3
     2 sets wires, extra RPs

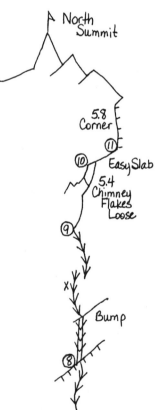

Fig. 14. *Bugaboo Spire, E Face/Cooper-Gran Route*

BUGABOO SPIRE

E Face, Left (Herr[2])
IV 5.10
Photos on pp. 60, 72
Protection:
 Standard rack to 4″
 Extra Friends, #2-#4

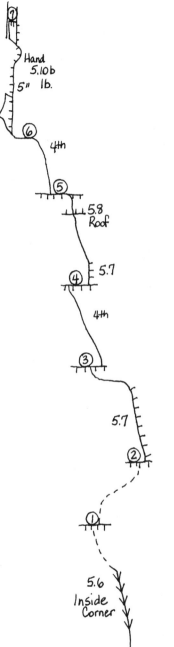

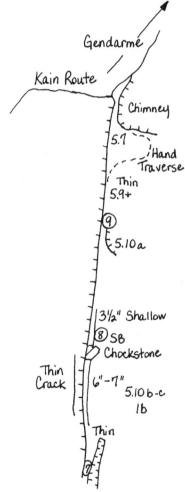

Fig. 15. Bugaboo Spire, E Face-Left/Herr[2]

small ledge. **4–6** Ascend hand cracks (stay to right) to a ledge (decent bivi). **7–8** Aid bolt ladder or face-climb right past two bolts (crux), then straight up and left to obtain upper dihedral (thin crack, often wet). **9–12** Easier climbing along shelves of flakes (some loose rock) and slabs to final steep corner (good cracks) and NE Ridge. Continue along ridge to N Summit. Generally a good route, although many cracks are flaring and incipient; can be climbed in one long day. *Time:* 1–2 days from base. *Descent:* Traverse summits and descend Kain Route.

J   East Face-Left/Herr[2]

IV   5.10 *(fig. 15) (photos, pp. 60, 72)*

Approach: Same as for Midnight Route. Climb snow to highest point directly below gendarme on S Ridge. Route follows a series of ledges and inside corners to a huge dihedral on left side of E Face to merge with S Ridge (Kain Route) below gendarme (see photo, p. 60). Variations are possible to get to the base of the huge dihedral (see fig. 15). **1–4** Climb moderately difficult inside corners and ledges (some Class 4) to steeper steps. **5–6** Ascend open book past roof to good ledge followed by Class 4 to base of huge dihedral. **7–10** Climb main dihedral, strenuous with two semi-hanging belay stances; crack widens to 7 inches on pitch 8 and narrows to a quarter inch on pitch 10; exit through short chimney to S Ridge (Kain Route). Continue on Kain Route past gendarme to S Summit. This route offers a very interesting alternative to attaining the S Summit, with the upper 4 pitches being high-quality climbing. *Time:* 6–7 hours from base. *Descent:* Same as for Kain Route.

SNOWPATCH SPIRE
10,050 ft. (3063 m)

Appearance and Location

Snowpatch Spire dominates the western skyline above Boulder Camp. The close proximity of its 2000-foot E Face to the Kain Hut gives one a false sense of scale. Its namesake, the small-looking snowfield that rests on the southeast shoulder, is actually over five acres in size. The elongated spire is dark from lichen stains and steep on all sides; it looks like a giant, ragged dorsal fin protruding from a glacial sea.

Snowpatch Spire viewed from the southwest

Although its sharp summit ridge aligns more with a true northwest-southeast direction, Snowpatch's faces are named after the major compass coordinates. The broad E Face towers above the lower Crescent Glacier with the first half (1000 feet) near vertical, while the upper half (1000 feet) leans at a less severe angle for the remaining distance to the twin summits.

The N Face is much smaller in area and slightly diamond shaped. It leans back toward the false north summit at about 70 degrees. The N Face is the southern sentinel tower of the Bugaboo-Snowpatch Col, maintaining a brooding aspect that is relaxed only when the afternoon sun shines between Pigeon and Howser spires to warm its fractured, slabby face.

The W Face cradles part of the upper Vowell Glacier. Vertical crack systems split this broad 1000-foot face every few feet. Several major aretes are separated by the dihedral or open book formations, which characterize this face. Two distinct summits distinguish Snowpatch's summit ridge-line, with the S Summit the highest point.

The S Face of Snowpatch has a true spirelike appearance. When viewed from the upper slopes of the Bugaboo Glacier, the triangular shape of the S Face reveals a broad base that plunges another 800 feet below the base of the W Face to the Bugaboo Glacier. The two sides of the triangular face extend upward at steep angles toward the sharp summit ridge. The SE Corner forms the eastern side and the W Face profile forms the other.

Notable First Ascents

When Conrad Kain made the first climbing reconnaissance of Snowpatch in 1916, he deemed it impossible to climb. Kain's claim and the failure of nine attempts during the next 24 years perpetuated the myth that Snowpatch was unclimbable. Raffi Bedayn, a Sierra activist in the late 1930s, reported that some skeptics went so far as to say that if they put Snowpatch in Yosemite Valley, it still would be many years before someone climbed it.

In 1938 Fritz Wiessner and Chappel Cranmer made a strong attempt, reaching a point below the foreboding black headwall above the snowpatch on the southwest shoulder. Deciding that the headwall would be predominantly aid, the pair quickly retreated. Wiessner later wrote that he was uninterested in "merely an affair of driving iron in virgin rock."

Finally, in August 1940, Jack Arnold and Bedayn completed what Wiessner and Cranmer had started; Snowpatch was the last major peak in the Bugaboo Group to be climbed. Arnold and Bedayn's route, the Southeast Corner (the easiest route on the rock to date) has since become a classic. With Snowpatch's unclimbable myth erased, other faces eventually fell to pioneer hardmen of the day.

Hans Kraus and James McCarthy were the first to climb the W Face in August 1956. They chose a direct line up one of the major dihedral formations that now bears their name. Originally rated 5.8/A1, this technical climb was one of the most difficult routes in the Bugaboo Group for several years.

In 1959, however, Fred Beckey and Hank Mather upped the ante when they established the first Grade VI in the Bugaboos. They did so with a successful climb of the untouched E Face of Snowpatch. Their success was partly attributed to the Yosemite-style tactics they employed on the big alpine face. They fixed ropes on the lower, steep section of the wall to provide an escape route in case of bad weather, until they were sure they could complete the route. Mostly aid, this multiday route still has seen few repeat ascents.

Although several other parties pioneered routes on Snowpatch's walls, none were as significant as the first free ascent of the E Face. Art Higbee, a climber from Colorado, who teamed up with David Breashears in 1975 to establish the first free route on the E Face of Snowpatch, called the Sunshine Wall (not to be confused with the Lowe-Scott route, called Sunshine, on the N Face). They climbed the 1800-foot route in one day. At the time, this feat was disputed, yet few have attempted to repeat it.

Climbing Snowpatch Spire

Snowpatch was made for climbing. Its graceful lines are lavishly endowed with countless vertical crack systems. The vertical fracturing of the peak lends itself to a variety of crack climbing techniques. The N and W faces offer the most free climbing. Much of the abrasive rock is clean, hard crystalline granite, with cracks that vary in size from thin finger-tip size to chimneys. Black lichen inhabits the rock where the violent forces of erosion have not scoured it, but this is an inconvenience only on new routes.

All climbs on Snowpatch are a challenge. Even the easiest route, the SE Corner, is long and quite sustained. No climb on this spire is less than a Grade IV in commitment. A few shorter routes on the W Face are often only a romp for experienced alpine rock climbers, but for sport climbers who are embarking on their first major alpine peak, Snowpatch can be a real education.

Few routes on Snowpatch have a free-climb rating of less than 5.9. But if you are comfortable at 5.9 or gymnastic grades harder than that, a whole climbing vacation could be spent on Snowpatch alone. The SW Ridge, the old Greenwood-Homer Route, and

Sunshine, a Lowe-Scott route on the N Face, are fine examples. These routes boast classic Bugaboo climbing with exposed belay stances and breathtaking views.

Standard modern protection racks are recommended. Cracks are often flared or parallel, so having some camming devices may be comforting. Unlike many crag routes, some routes wander a bit, so bring additional slings and long runners. An ice axe and roped travel on glaciers are advisable safety precautions for all approaches. Crampons may be necessary for the Bugaboo-Snowpatch Col late in the season.

Approach the E and N faces via the Crescent Glacier, and the S Face via the Bugaboo Glacier. All are relatively easy hikes, but crevasse danger exists on all glaciers. Approach the W Face by crossing the Bugaboo-Snowpatch Col to the upper Vowell Glacier. See fig. 1 for locations.

All descents are by rappel. See the topo drawings and marked photos for locations. Several major rappel routes are maintained: S Summit (Kraus-McCarthy Route, W Face), N Summit (Beckey-Greenwood Route, W Face), and Sunshine on the N Face. Rappel stations should be regarded with caution. Anchors, slings, and rappel rings may need to be replaced or backed-up for safety. Use discretion and good judgment and be prepared to contribute to the anchor system if necessary.

Route Descriptions

SOUTHEAST SHOULDER

A   Southeast Corner

IV   5.6+ *(fig. 16) (photo, p. 111)*

Approach: When looking at the SE Shoulder from Kain Hut, a prominent notch in the lower buttress marks the beginning of the route. However, access is best attained from the south side of the spire from the Bugaboo Glacier. Ascend medial moraine (separating Crescent and Bugaboo glaciers) above Kain Hut to the base of the shoulder's lower buttress. Traverse south and west (sometimes on snow and ice) around buttress to gully (marked by several low-angle dihedral formations on left) that leads to notch in shoulder (1 hour). Scramble to notch (several variations may be climbed to the ridge crest via low-angled dihedrals to the left, 5.6–5.10). **1–3** From notch scramble left to slab below wall split by large corner. **4–5** Ascend large low-angle corners to roof (Wiessner overhang). **6** Hand traverse right around roof to upper slab at base of large snowpatch. **7–11** Friction climb slab along left side of snowpatch. **12–13** Move right and behind large detached block to base of headwall. **14** Ascend cracks up and left

SNOWPATCH SPIRE

SE Corner
IV 5.6+
Photo on p. 111
Protection:
    Standard rack to 4"
    Extra slings

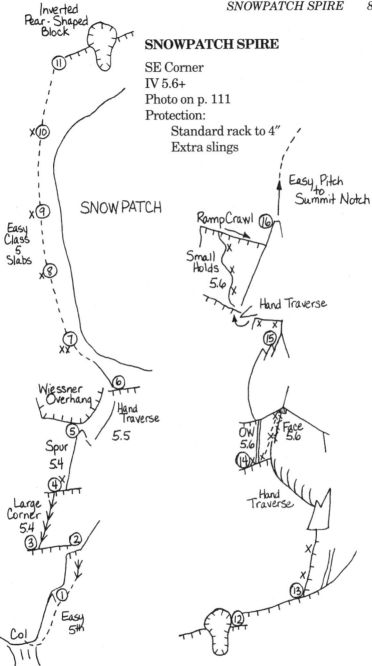

Fig. 16. *Snowpatch Spire, SE Corner*

to steep wall split with offwidth on left and vertical quartz dike on right. **15** Offwidth on left can be "strong-armed" (when dry) or dike on right can be "finessed" by face-climbing straight up; move left and climb crack to hornlike flakes. **16** Climb straight up 10 feet, then hand traverse left and follow zig-zag crack up and left to ramp; move right on ramp to horn. **17** Easy Class 5 climbing leads to summit slabs. *Time:* 6–7 hours from Kain Hut. *Descent:* Rappel Kraus-McCarthy Route, W Face.

B   Variation: Direct Finish

5.9

Same as normal SE Corner Route but go left at pear-shaped block (see topo) and ascend a left-slanting break through the initial part of the upper headwall. Climb chimney and move left onto main buttress around large chockstone (120 feet). Easier climbing leads to a short, flaring crack (wide) and a large ledge (120 feet, 5.7). Avoid large overhang at right corner of ledge by climbing 10 feet up a crack on the wall to another ledge. Climb right into a corner and past an overhang into a chimney to belay below another roof (70 feet, 5.9). Climb easier crack to left and gain crack in large boulder that leads to summit ridge.

C   Lightning Bolt Crack

5.10 *(fig. 17)*

Approach: Same as for SE Corner. Move left several hundred feet to huge, Z-shaped right-slanting dihedral. **1–3** Climb dihedral, undercling roof (crux), and continue up corner until possible to exit left on ramp to rotten gully. *Time:* 2–3 hours from Kain Hut. *Descent:* Down-climb rotten gully.

SOUTH FACE

(photo, p. 84)

Approach: Same as for SE Corner, but continue farther W up the Bugaboo Glacier to S Face (1 hour).

D   South Face-Upper Section

V   5.8/A2 or 5.11 *(fig. 18) (photo, p. 84)*

Several hundred feet east of center is a series of ledges and ramps. Scramble Class 4 and some easy Class 5 left on ramps to base of upper wall, approximately 500 feet above glacier (several hours). **1–2** Climb steep, right-slanting parallel crack system. **3–4** Climb left past flakes to another crack system. **5–7** Work slightly left by climbing short steps to nice ledges; finish on SW Ridge to summit.

Time: 1–1.5 days. *Descent:* Rappel Kraus-McCarthy Route, W Face.

E   South Face Direct

V   5.8/A2 *(photo, p. 84)*

At center of lower face, climb direct line that merges with upper route at large platform (500 feet). Details unclear, but pitches involve much technical aid and are time consuming. Continue up face to finish on S Face-Upper. *Time:* 2 days from base to top. *Descent:* Rappel Kraus-McCarthy Route, W Face.

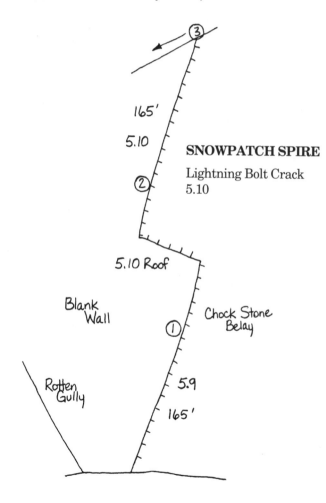

Fig. 17. *Snowpatch Spire, Lightning Bolt Crack*

Snowpatch Spire, S Face

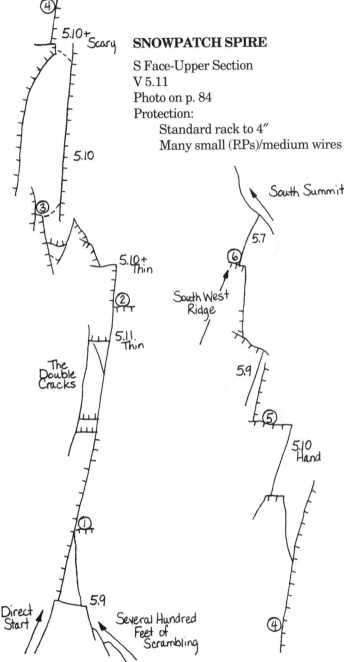

SNOWPATCH SPIRE

S Face-Upper Section
V 5.11
Photo on p. 84
Protection:
Standard rack to 4″
Many small (RPs)/medium wires

Fig. 18. Snowpatch Spire, S Face-Upper Section

F South Face-Left

V 5.8/A3 *(photo, p. 84)*

About 200 feet west of the S Face Direct Route is a major corner system at lower left side of face. **1–3** Free-climb prominent flakes in corner to right-slanting crack. Follow slanting crack until it is possible to go straight up. Account and number of pitches unclear; ascend many technical aid pitches on poor rock to Surf's Up Ledge on the SW Ridge. Continue climbing SW Ridge to summit. ***Time:*** 2 days from base to top. ***Descent:*** Rappel Kraus-McCarthy Route, W Face.

WEST FACE

(photo, p. 87)

Approach: Via Crescent Glacier and Bugaboo-Snowpatch Col to upper Vowell Glacier (1–2 hours).

G Southwest Ridge

III 5.8+ *(fig. 19) (photo, p. 87)*

Traverse W Face to south end. Scramble 200 feet to base of crack/flake system that eventually leads up to SW Shoulder. **1–3** Climb flakes and flaring cracks (rounded) to alcove. **4** Move right and climb (grunt) over blocks and down-climb to airy Surf's Up Ledge above the S Face. **5–7** Choose cracks or chimney system to summit ridge; excellent climbing in a very exposed position. ***Time:*** 4–5 hours from base. ***Descent:*** Rappel Kraus-McCarthy Route, W Face.

H Variation: Southwest Ridge-Direct Finish

5.9 *(fig. 19) (photo, p. 87)*

Climb first three pitches of SW Ridge to alcove. **4** From alcove, move left and follow corner system to blocky ledge. **5–6** Climb crack to ledge, then move right and climb easy flakes and cracks to summit ridge.

I Attack of the Killer Chipmunks

III 5.9 *(photo, p. 87)*

Scramble up scree-strewn ramp to about 50 feet left of the SW Ridge Route. **1–3** Climb flakes and cracks, following line through wide crack/chimney system. **4–6** Continue following wide cracks to left-facing corner capped by roof (5.9). Original account un-

Snowpatch Spire, W Face (note climber at base)

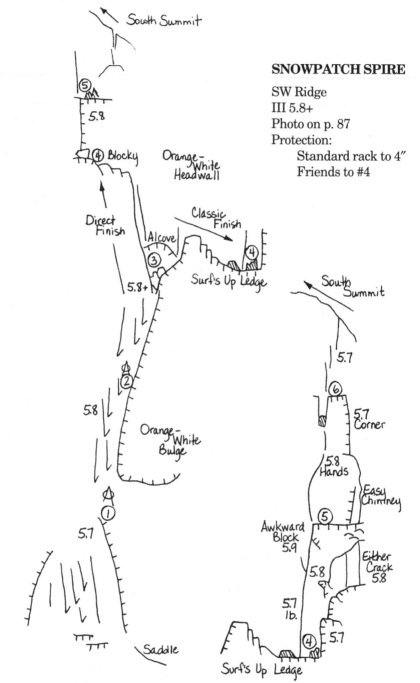

SNOWPATCH SPIRE

SW Ridge
III 5.8+
Photo on p. 87
Protection:
    Standard rack to 4″
    Friends to #4

Fig. 19. *Snowpatch Spire, SW Ridge and Direct Finish*

clear. **Time:** 4–5 hours from base. **Descent:** Rappel Kraus-McCarthy Route, W Face.

J Degringolade

III 5.9+ *(photo, p. 87)*

Route follows a line up major open book formation to summit ridge at notch just south of S Summit. **1–2** Scramble Class 4 ground for 200 feet, then climb to short chimney and move out left to ledge. **3–4** Climb groove and cracks to ledges; climb flakes past strenuous undercling to poor stance at small grassy ledge. **5** Move right to dirty inside corner; climb and undercling past flake to ledge. At ledge, cross large gully/crack system to gain good ledge. **6–8** Climb inside corner above belay to bulge; follow crack right into chimney behind flake to top of small pinnacle. Continue up corner to hand traverse right to gain awkward slot and ramp to good stance. Continue up easy ground to S Summit. **Time:** 3–4 hours from base. **Descent:** Rappel Kraus-McCarthy Route, W Face.

K Variation: Rock the Casbah

5.9 *(fig. 20)*

Scramble past Killer Chipmunks Route to triangular-shaped black pinnacle that leans against the lower wall. **1–2** Climb right side of small pinnacle and face-climb to ledge with spike-shaped block. **3–5** Follow flakes straight up until it is possible to down-climb a short chimney to top of large block. **6–7** From top of block, step right and face-climb black slab to grooves with overlaps; continue up grooves and slot to summit ridge.

L Which Way Route

IV 5.10 *(fig. 21) (photo, p. 87)*

Starts same as Rock the Casbah first pitch, but angles left and joins Furry Pink for last two pitches. **1–2** Climb to top of small pinnacle and face-climb up and left to ledge. **3–6** Continue to follow flakes as wall steepens; ascend crack that splits slab and finish thin crack leading directly to the Furry Pink arete. One sling belay, but most belay stances are good. Sustained, strenuous climbing on good rock. **Time:** 5–7 hours from base. **Descent:** Rappel Kraus-McCarthy Route, W Face.

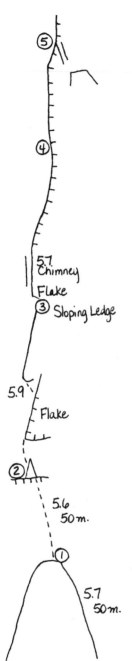

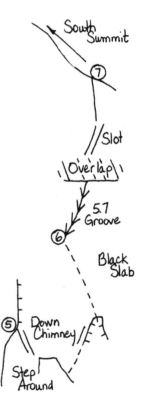

SNOWPATCH SPIRE

Rock the Casbah
III 5.9
Protection:
    Standard rack to 3 1/2″

Fig. 20. *Snowpatch Spire, Rock the Casbah*

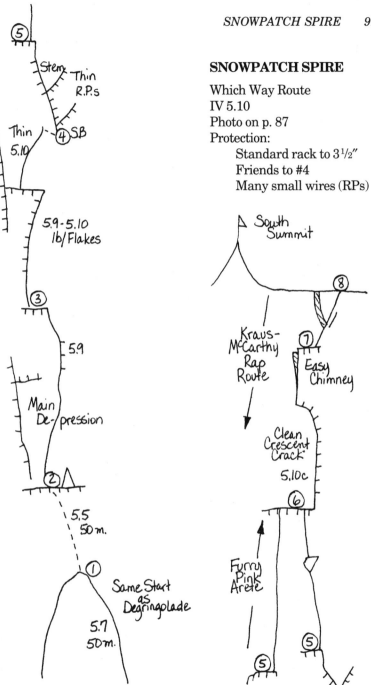

SNOWPATCH SPIRE

Which Way Route
IV 5.10
Photo on p. 87
Protection:
    Standard rack to $3\frac{1}{2}''$
    Friends to #4
    Many small wires (RPs)

Fig. 21. *Snowpatch Spire, Which Way Route*

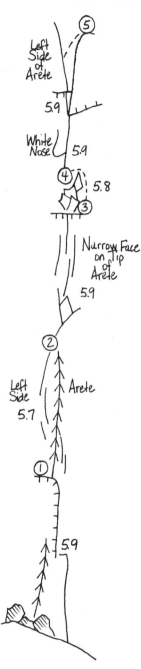

SNOWPATCH SPIRE

Furry Pink
IV 5.10c
Photo on p. 87
Protection:
    2 sets Friends to #4
    1 set wires

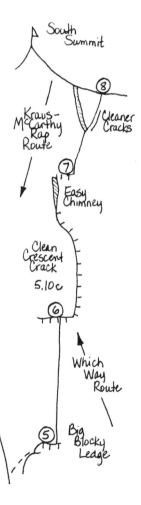

Fig. 22. *Snowpatch Spire, Furry Pink*

M   Furry Pink

IV   5.10c *(fig. 22) (photo, p. 87)*

This climb follows the pink-colored arete, furry with lichen in spots, that leads directly to the main false S Summit, right of the Kraus-McCarthy Route. **1–3** Start climb in crack just right of lower arete crest, then, more or less follow the arete to a big blocky ledge. **4–6** Angle up and right a short pitch past blocks, then climb past white "nose" up left side of arete to second big blocky ledge; climb nice straight-in crack to ledge below (crux) crescent crack. **7–8** Lieback and undercling crescent flake/crack to easy chimney and continue up easier cracks to summit. Sustained, high-quality climbing on good rock. *Time:* 5–7 hours from base. *Descent:* Rappel Kraus-McCarthy Route, W Face.

N   Kraus-McCarthy Route

IV   5.8+ *(fig. 23) (photo, p. 87)*

A major open book/gully formation 150 feet south (right) of the S Summit marks the general line of ascent. Originally climbed using aid to surmount the bulging overhang on pitch 6, this moderately strenuous route is usually free-climbed now. It is considered the best descent route from the S Summit. Scramble 200 feet to base of main corner system. **1–3** Begin climbing flakes that slant right until it is possible to move left and assault a roof near left edge of gully. **4–7** Climb easy flake/ramp that slants right, gradually work up center of gully until it narrows to chimney. **8** Climb chimney until it narrows to offwidth, move right and climb hand crack on right wall to summit ridge. *Time:* 5–6 hours from base. *Descent:* Rappel route, double ropes recommended.

O   Wildflowers

IV   5.9 *(fig. 24) (photo, p. 87)*

Directly below the S Summit a large pinnacle leans against the W Face. Route follows dihedral formed by left edge of pinnacle, in direct line to summit. **1–2** Easy climbing follows natural line to left edge and base of pinnacle. **3–5** Climb main corner system, grooves and cracks on left-facing wall to top of tower. **6** Follow solitary crack to summit. A fine route, with character and good protection. *Time:* 4–5 hours from base. *Descent:* Rappel Kraus-McCarthy Route, W Face.

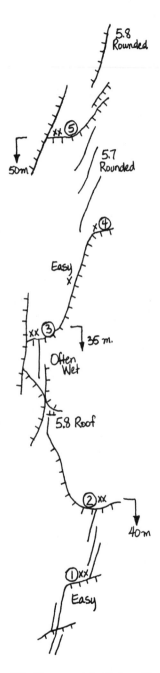

SNOWPATCH SPIRE

Kraus/McCarthy Route
IV 5.8+
Photo on p. 87
Protection:
    Standard rack to 3″
    1 set Friends to #3½

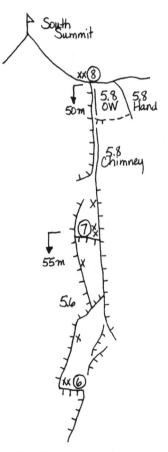

Fig. 23. *Snowpatch Spire, Kraus-McCarthy Route*

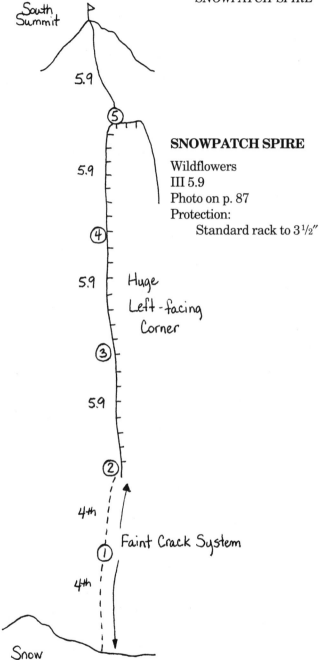

SNOWPATCH SPIRE

Wildflowers
III 5.9
Photo on p. 87
Protection:
 Standard rack to 3½″

Fig. 24. Snowpatch Spire, Wildflowers

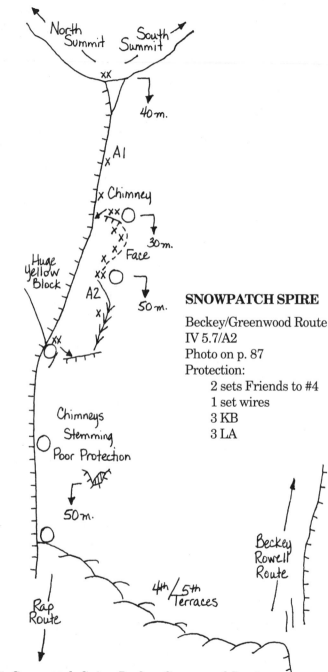

SNOWPATCH SPIRE

Beckey/Greenwood Route
IV 5.7/A2
Photo on p. 87
Protection:
    2 sets Friends to #4
    1 set wires
    3 KB
    3 LA

Fig. 25. *Snowpatch Spire, Beckey-Greenwood Route*

P Beckey-Rowell Route

IV 5.8/A4 *(photo, p. 87)*

Route follows huge dihedral that cleaves wall just north (left) of S Summit. The route originally involved several sections of hard aid (A3–A4), but variations to the right are said to offer easier free-climbing possibilities to 5.9 (descriptions unclear, possibly Wildflowers Route). **1–3** Moderate climbing to comfortable ledge (here it is possible to follow flakes that angle right to gain Wildflowers). **4–5** Long pitches follow dihedral to hanging belay below and right of "Y" crack. **6–8** To avoid roof in upper dihedral, tension right several times to better cracks that lead to overhanging summit block (marginal nailing at times in bottoming cracks). **9** Traverse right edge of block on narrow ledge to opposite side and summit. *Time:* 8–9 hours from base. *Descent:* Rappel Kraus-McCarthy Route.

Q Beckey-Greenwood Route

IV 5.7/A2 *(fig. 25) (photo, p. 87)*

Start same as for Beckey-Rowell Route, then angle left on Class 4 and easy Class 5 several hundred feet along terraces to gain main dihedral characterized by huge white/yellow block at top left. At terrace/dihedral intersection, climb two strenuous pitches in corner, stem and chimney to base of huge yellow block. Tension right to ledge where next two pitches climb right wall to avoid chimney in main corner. Regain corner for final pitch to central notch in summit ridge. Take broken crest to N Summit. *Time:* 9–11 hours from base. *Descent:* Rappel same route (best descent from N Summit).

R Tam-Tam Boom-Boom Pili-Pili

IV 5.11/A1 *(fig. 26) (photo, p. 87)*

This route starts several hundred feet left (north) of Beckey-Rowell Route and crosses the Beckey-Greenwood Route on the terraces ascending a direct line to the tower north of the S Summit. **1–2** Climb crack to shallow corner system (thin crack, crux) that turns into a chimney below the terraces. **3–4** Cross terraces and climb another corner system (left-facing) around prominent flake. **5–6** Face-climb to large, clean, right-slanting dihedral that points to S Summit. **7** Continue climbing corner system to top of tower. Follow summit ridge to S Summit tower and traverse onto E Face slabs to gain summit. *Time:* 7–8 hours from base. *Descent:* Rappel Kraus-McCarthy Route.

SNOWPATCH SPIRE

Tam-Tam Boom-Boom Pili-Pili
IV 5.11/A1
Photo on p. 87
Protection:
  2 sets Friends to #4
  2 sets wires
  3 KB
  3 LA

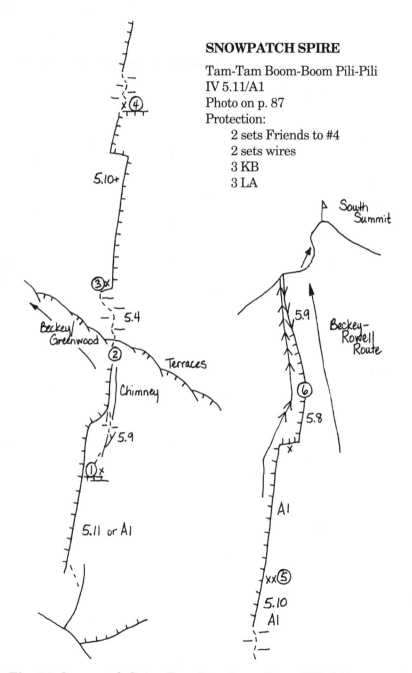

Fig. 26. Snowpatch Spire, Tam-Tam Boom-Boom Pili-Pili

SNOWPATCH SPIRE

Tower Arete
IV 5.10–/A2
Photo on p. 87
Protection:
    2 sets Friends to #4
    1 set wires, extra RPs
    4 KB, tie-offs
    2 LA

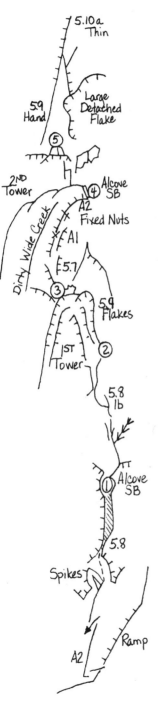

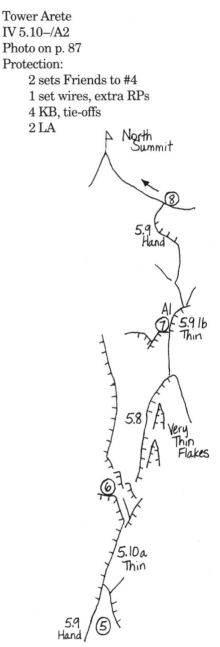

Fig. 27. *Snowpatch Spire, Tower Arete*

S   Tower Arete

IV   5.10–/A2 *(fig. 27) (photo, p. 87)*

Several pinnacles distinguish the face directly below the N Summit. Line follows cracks up right side of towers. **1–2** Aid very thin cracks through roofs to alcove; free-climb easier ground to rounded flakes that form tower. **3–4** Climb to top of tower, traverse left to gain arching flake/cracks (wide dirt-filled crack farther left possibly key to free-bypass here); aid past black roof (4-inch flaring crack) to alcove belay. **5–6** Easy Class 5 blocks lead to ledge at base of large detached flake; jam hand-size crack (parallel and flaring) that thins to finger-size. **7–8** From comfortable belay, angle right onto very thin flakes and climb to awkward belay; grunt over bulge to gain upper hand cracks (covered with black lichen) that top-out 50 feet south of N Summit. A good climb that could possibly go free. *Time:* 7–8 hours from base. *Descent:* Rappel Beckey-Greenwood Route.

T   North Summit Direct

IV   5.8/A2 or 5.11+ *(fig. 28) (photo, p. 87)*

This route follows a long right-slanting parallel crack system through white rock directly to the N Summit. Start several hundred feet north of Tower Arete in a chimney formed by a detached flake. **1–2** Chimney through flakes to right-facing corner capped by obvious roof. **3–5** Move left and follow steep right-facing shallow corners (cracks are flaring and parallel, thin-hand to thin-fingertip). **6–7** From sling belay, work left into good hand crack to easier ground and summit. This route is very aesthetic in directness and appearance, albeit sustained and strenuous. *Time:* 7–8 hours from base. *Descent:* Rappel Beckey-Greenwood Route.

U   Flamingo Fling

IV   5.9 *(fig. 29) (photo, p. 87)*

Line parallels North Summit Direct Route, several hundred feet north. Various starts are possible to gain main flake system comprising lower third of route. **1–2** Moderate Class 5 leads to long broken section just below flake system. **3–5** Lieback and jam flake/cracks to good ledge. **6–7** Climb steep crack that widens from hands to fists. From sling belay below small roof, climb crack that widens from finger-size to chimney in one pitch. **8–9** Easier cracks lead to Flamingo Flake; climb left side of large flake and follow easy ramp to summit. Good climb with variety of crack-climbing challenges. *Time:* 6–7 hours from base. *Descent:* Rappel Beckey-Greenwood Route.

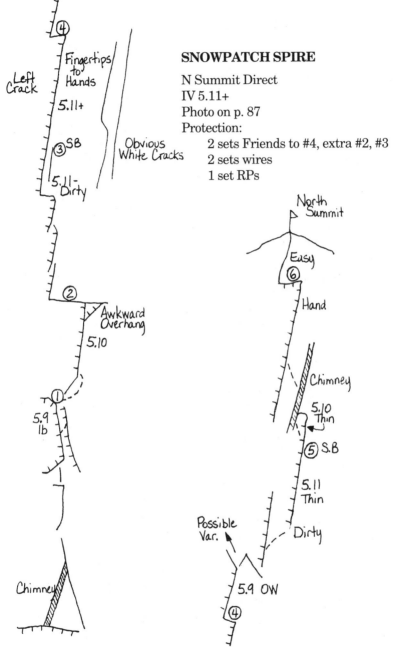

SNOWPATCH SPIRE

N Summit Direct
IV 5.11+
Photo on p. 87
Protection:
  2 sets Friends to #4, extra #2, #3
  2 sets wires
  1 set RPs

Fig. 28. *Snowpatch Spire, N Summit Direct*

Snowpatch Spire, N Face

SNOWPATCH SPIRE

Flamingo Fling
IV 5.9
Photo on p. 87
Protection:
    Standard rack to 3½″
    1 set Friends to #4

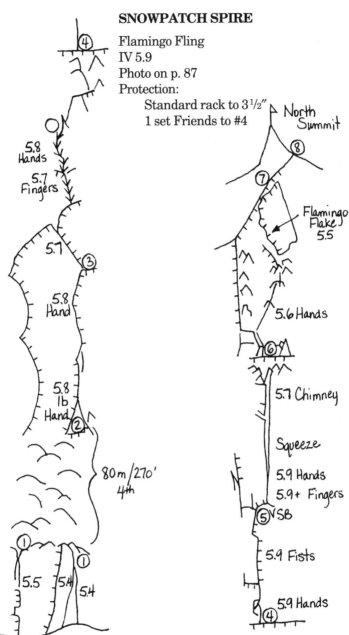

Fig. 29. *Snowpatch Spire, Flamingo Fling*

V   Quasimodo

IV   5.9/A1 *(photo, p. 87)*

Start same as for Gran-Hudson Route; scramble (Class 4) through broken section to base of large chimney system. **1–2** From belay in alcove, move right, then down 10 feet to gain cracks that pass through small roof (5.8). Work right to belay. **3–5** Lieback (5.5) to where crack widens to 10 inches. Climb offwidth (5.8) to belay. **6–7** Move right and ascend right-leaning crack to overhanging flake/chimney (5.8). Hand traverse left to gain blocky section and belay. Climb cracks on white wall to roof (5.9). Pendulum right twice on fixed pins to gain easier blocky ground (A1/5.7). **8–10** Easy Class 5 leads to large ledge below chimney (5.4). Climb broken flakes above chimney and go slightly right to belay (5.6). Lieback crack (5.8), then move left to boulder. Finish by working right to lieback crack (5.5) and summit. *Time:* 6–7 hours from base. ***Descent:*** Rappel Beckey-Greenwood Route.

W   Gran-Hudson Route

IV   5.7/A2 *(photo, p. 87)*

The left-most groove in the W Face marks this line of ascent. It follows a long prominent chimney to the notch just north of N Summit. Start 200 feet below and right of main chimney. **1–3** Work left past flakes to gain broken section below chimney. **4–5** Chimney two 100-foot pitches working left to gain main chimney. **6–7** Chimney to chockstone (100 feet) and bypass to right (80 feet). **8** Ascend straightforward pitch to notch on summit ridge; join Buckingham Route to N Summit. *Time:* 7–8 hours from base. ***Descent:*** Rappel Beckey-Greenwood Route.

X   Northwest Corner/Buckingham Route

IV   5.6/A2 *(photo, p. 87)*

Near Bugaboo-Snowpatch Col, a groove system cuts the northwest edge of the W Face toward a "yellow tower" that marks the top of the N Face. This was the first route to the N Summit. The number of pitches and route details are unclear. Ascend several pitches of cracks and flakes to base of yellow tower. Surmount short roof to gain right-slanting dike (parallels ridge). Follow dike/chimney 200 feet, then climb three pitches of moderate Class 5 (5.4) past flakes and cracks to where dike merges with smooth wall (5.8 friction variations left are possible here). Aid (2 bolts) to ledge. Traverse left (aid) to lieback that leads to easier ground and top of second tower. Rappel into sharp notch (top of Gran-Hudson chimney), then traverse left (aid) around corner to vertical dihedral (**variation:** instead of rappelling into notch, rappel

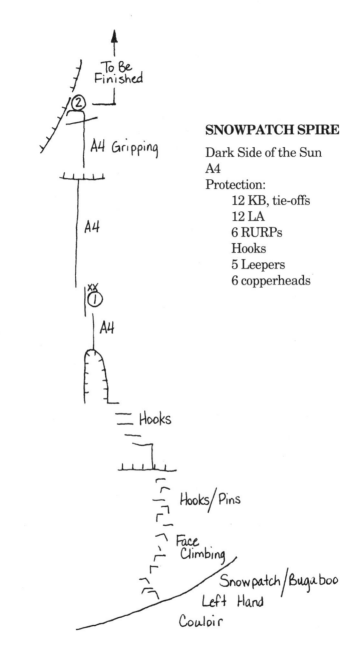

To Be Finished

②

A4 Gripping

A4

A4

①

A4

Hooks

Hooks/Pins

Face Climbing

Snowpatch/Bugaboo Left Hand Couloir

SNOWPATCH SPIRE

Dark Side of the Sun
A4
Protection:
    12 KB, tie-offs
    12 LA
    6 RURPs
    Hooks
    5 Leepers
    6 copperheads

Fig. 30. Snowpatch Spire, Dark Side of the Sun

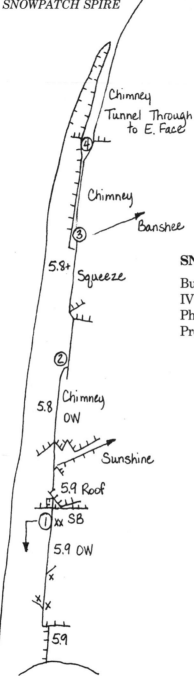

Chimney
Tunnel Through
to E. Face

④

Chimney

Banshee

③

5.8+ Squeeze

②

5.8 Chimney
OW

Sunshine

5.9 Roof

① xx SB

5.9 OW

5.9

SNOWPATCH SPIRE

Bugaboo Corner
IV 5.10–
Photo on p. 102
Protection:
    Standard rack to 4″
    Extra to 8″

Fig. 31. *Snowpatch Spire, Bugaboo Corner*

ice-choked chimney to gain dihedral climbed by first ascent party—this is preferred to original line). Aid corner until possible to free-climb (5.6) to base of final tower. Scramble to N Summit via slabs on E Face. *Time:* 8–9 hours from base. *Descent:* Rappel Beckey-Greenwood Route.

NORTH FACE

(photo, p. 102)

Approach: Via Crescent Glacier to Bugaboo-Snowpatch Col.

Y   Dark Side of the Sun

A4 *(fig. 30)*

This incomplete two-pitch aid route works up the lower slab on the west side of the N Face. **1** Hook crystals (ground fall possible, no protection possible to hold a fall) through roof and nail incipient crack above flake to sling belay . **2** Nail thin crack to small stance. Possible finish for route leads up to better cracks and large clean, white dihedral that merges with Banshee higher on wall. *Time:* 4 hours from base. *Descent:* Rappel same route.

Z   Bugaboo Corner

IV   5.9/A1 or 5.10– *(fig. 31) (photo, p. 102)*

From the Bugaboo-Snowpatch Col, the N Face is split on the left (east) edge by a widening crack. Ascend lower snow slopes of col to easy ledges and base of crack system. **1–2** Jam hand crack through roof to gain slab where crack gradually widens to offwidth; continue in wide crack (small cracks nearby or inside offwidth offer good protection). **3–4** Grunt up wide crack to squeeze and finally chimney-size (good cracks inside for small- to medium-size protection). **5–12** Tunnel behind obvious flake to E Face; cross Tom Egan, Sunshine Wall, and join upper Parker-Brashaw Route to finish at N Summit. Classic crack climb that compares with Steck-Salathe Route on Sentinel Rock, Yosemite. *Time:* 8–10 hours from base. *Descent:* Rappel same route or from N Summit—Beckey-Greenwood Route, W Face.

AA   Banshee

IV   5.10 *(fig. 32)*

This major variant of Bugaboo Corner traverses slabs at mid-height on wall following line of least resistance and finishing on "yellow tower" (top of N Face). **1–3** Same as for Bugaboo Corner. **3–5** Traverse up and right by friction and cracks to avoid major roofs; climb corner to gain upper slab and final solitary crack to

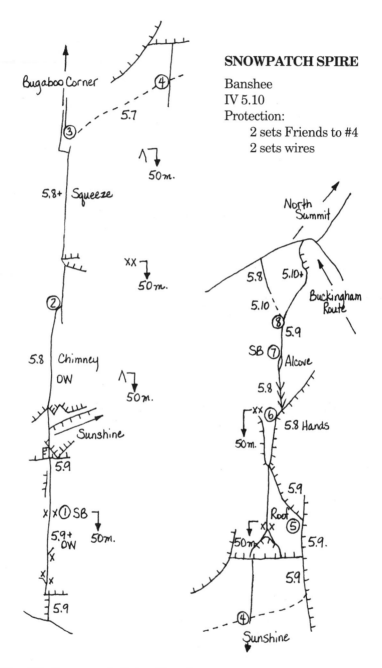

SNOWPATCH SPIRE

Banshee
IV 5.10
Protection:
  2 sets Friends to #4
  2 sets wires

Fig. 32. *Snowpatch Spire, Banshee*

SNOWPATCH SPIRE

Sunshine
IV 5.10+
Photo on p. 102
Protection:
2 sets Friends to #4
2 sets wires, extra RPs

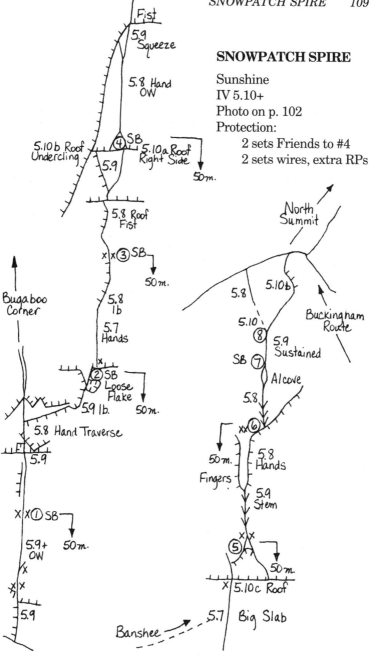

Fig. 33. *Snowpatch Spire, Sunshine*

summit. **6–8** Climb flakes to gain main crack system. Follow solitary crack to obvious "Y" fork near top. Take left crack to top of tower. *Time:* 6–7 hours from base. *Descent:* Rappel Sunshine Route, N Face.

BB   Sunshine

IV   5.10+ *(fig. 33) (photo, p. 102)*

Not to be confused with the Sunshine Wall, E Face, this route is a direct line that takes on all major difficulties (roofs) that Banshee avoids. **1** Same as for Bugaboo Corner. **2** At serrated roof a hand-raillike traverse is possible to gain another major crack system that splits the middle of the face. **3–5** Jam and lieback crack to major roof; left (cleaner but sometimes wet) or right variations are possible (similar difficulty). From belay above roof, continue jamming widening crack to squeeze that leads to another tier of slabs split by a solitary crack. Jam crack through left side of next major roof (good finger locks over lip). **6–7** Climb flakes and move left from ramp to follow main solitary crack. **8–9** Jam crack for two sustained pitches of high-quality climbing to top of tower. With generous portions of classic, sustained 5.8 crack climbing that is spiced with short challenging sections and many sling belays, this route is possibly one of the finest climbs in the Bugaboos even though it does not go to a summit. Although shadowed and cool in the morning, by early afternoon (midsummer) the sun reaches the base of the wall. A late start makes it possible to race the shadow line up the wall before sunset. *Time:* 6–7 hours from base. *Descent:* Rappel same route; slings and rap rings may need to be replaced.

EAST FACE

(photo, p. 111)

Approach: Via Crescent Glacier above Kain Hut.

CC   Hobo's Haven

IV   5.7/A4 *(fig. 34) (photo, p. 111)*

This route ascends difficult aid cracks to the top of the slight pinnacle formed by flakes along the lower northeast corner of the E Face. **1–2** Scramble from Crescent Glacier to steep ramp that leads to overhanging flakes. Nail and hook major flake/corner to gain vertical crack. **3–4** Nail crack to roof, difficult aid moves to right end at blank section. Hook crystals to gain crack system that leads to left-slanting crack below main pinnacle. **5–6** Con-

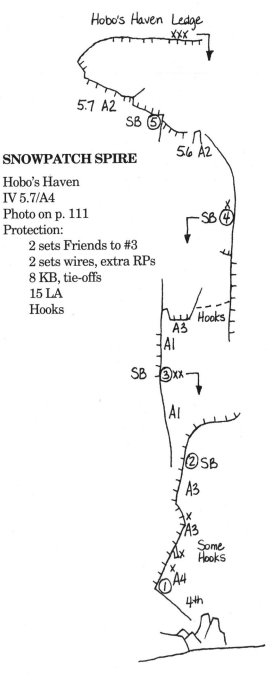

SNOWPATCH SPIRE

Hobo's Haven
IV 5.7/A4
Photo on p. 111
Protection:
    2 sets Friends to #3
    2 sets wires, extra RPs
    8 KB, tie-offs
    15 LA
    Hooks

Fig. 34. *Snowpatch Spire, Hobo's Haven*

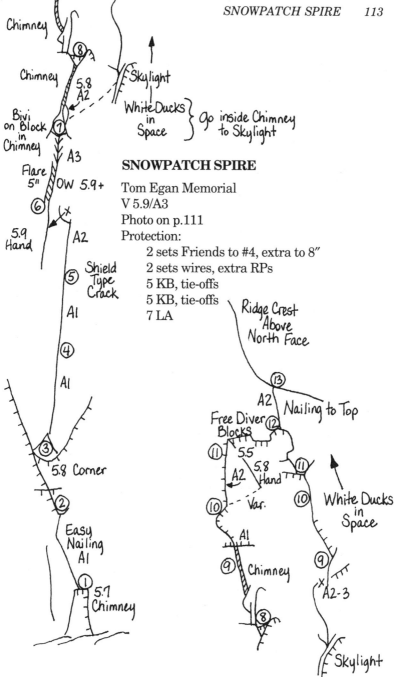

SNOWPATCH SPIRE

Tom Egan Memorial
V 5.9/A3
Photo on p.111
Protection:
 2 sets Friends to #4, extra to 8″
 2 sets wires, extra RPs
 5 KB, tie-offs
 5 KB, tie-offs
 7 LA

Fig. 35. *Snowpatch Spire, Tom Egan Memorial and White Ducks in Space*

tinue aiding slanting crack with occasional free moves to top of pinnacle. *Time:* 7–8 hours from base. *Descent:* Rappel same route.

DD   Tom Egan Memorial

V   5.9/A3 *(fig. 35) (photo, p. 111)*

This route ascends cracks through a light-colored headwall (similar to the Shield on El Capitan in Yosemite) on the far northern end of the W Face. Scramble broken area above the Crescent Glacier to large flake that leans against the wall. **1–3** Chimney behind flake and aid left-leaning flake system to ledge. **4–6** Aid steep, clean, finger-size crack (small camming devices helpful). Pendulum left and climb 3-inch crack to ledge at base of offwidth. **7–8** Follow main crack line, often liebacking blocks inside chimney, and squeeze through slot to ledge near skylight (top of Bugaboo Corner flake). Here it is possible to chimney right for White Ducks in Space Variation (5 pitches, 5.7/A3, see fig. 35). **9–11** Move left and chimney to gain aid cracks in right-facing corner to "Free-diver blocks." **12–13** Traverse blocks right and aid crack to ridge crest. Finish on Buckingham to N Summit or descend N Face en rappel. A high-quality aid route that may be free-climbed someday. *Time:* 2 days. *Descent:* Rappel Beckey-Greenwood Route, W Face, or rappel Sunshine, N Face.

EE   Variation: White Ducks in Space

5.7/A3 *(fig. 35) (photo, p. 111)*

9–11 From skylight, aid (A3) crescent-shaped flake and roof to large ledge. **12** Climb (free/aid) cracks to sloping ramp and follow crack above for 80 feet to ridge.

FF   Sunshine Wall

IV   5.10– *(fig. 36) (photo, p. 111)*

A long black streak on the lower third of the wall directly below the N Summit marks the start for this route. This route follows a series of flakes and ledges that angle right and then traverse toward the Tom Egan headwall before taking a direct line to summit ridge 200 feet south of Tom Egan finish. **1–5** Climb flakes of good rock that angle right; some down-climbing required in traverse section (cracks up to 6 inches). **6–8** Jam overhanging hand crack with good footholds to long chimney (160 feet, no protection), squeeze out of chimney to gain thin crack in dihedral. **9–11** Climb short vertical steps to gain ridge crest. Continue up Buckingham Route to N Summit. Compares with S Buttress of Mt. Moran; good route with bold runouts. *Time:* 10–12 hours

SNOWPATCH SPIRE

Sunshine Wall
V 5.10–
Photo on p. 111
Protection:
    2 sets Friends to #4, extra to 8″
    1 set wires
    extra slings

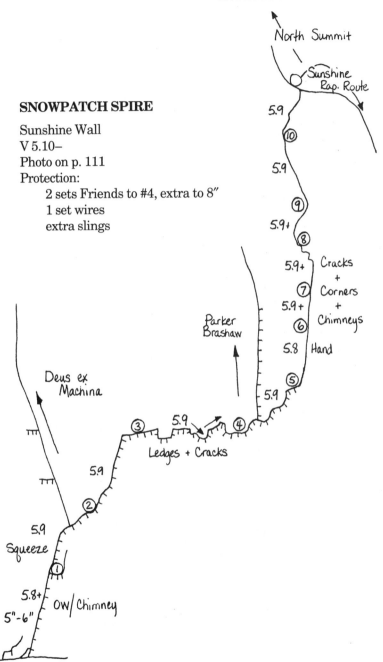

Fig. 36. Snowpatch Spire, Sunshine Wall

from base. **Descent:** Rappel Beckey-Greenwood Route, W Face, or rappel Sunshine, N Face.

GG   Variation: Parker-Brashaw Route

V   5.9/A1 *(photo, p. 111)*

Start same as for Sunshine Wall. Route deviates near end of traverse (pitch 5) and ascends directly toward ice-filled gully/notch north of N Summit. **1–4** Climb Sunshine Wall Route. Ascend overhanging, black, left-facing open book. Continue climbing cracks and corners to below ice-filled gully. Traverse diagonally left and climb cracks and corners just left of south wall of gully to N Summit. Very reasonable alternative to unprotected chimneys on Sunshine Wall Route, but exact details of route are unclear.

HH   Deus ex Machina

VI   5.9/A2 *(fig. 37) (photo, p. 111)*

Start same as for Sunshine Wall; at pitch 2, route takes left-leaning crack through lower section of face then ascends a plumb line directly toward N Summit. **1–2** Climb Sunshine Wall Route to intersection with obvious left-leaning crack. **3–6** Aid crack with occasional free moves past good belay ledges to highest ledge, nail loose flake. Move right to corner and nail cracks past roofs. Move to left edge of large dark roof, aid roof to series of ramps (60 feet below larger roof); sling belay. **7–9** Climb series of strenuous overhanging corners, aid above alcove, then free-climb low-angle gully to good ledge. Aid left-leaning corner to ledge. **10–13** Move down/left, nail 30-foot pillar, traverse down/left, and step across to crack system. Climb to double cracks and flakes in right-facing corner below chimney. Go left into chimney and up 30 feet. Aid right crack to belay ledge. Climb flaky roof to right-facing corner, belay in black flared corner. **14–16** Move left; face-climb ramp to flared corner. Climb wide crack (3–4 inches) in low-angled corner to 70 feet below summit block. Class 3 friction to summit. **Time:** 2–3 days. **Descent:** Rappel Beckey-Greenwood Route, W Face.

Variation:

3 From ledge above pitch 2, chimney 20 feet (5.9) and climb slab to top of block. **4–5** Step left and climb thin crack to flakes on right wall (5.10+), mixed free and aid up overhanging crack to sloping ledge. Climb right diagonally (5.6) in groove then left to flake and ledge. **6–7** Move left to lieback (5.8) to ledge. Traverse left to roof; aid past and rejoin regular route.

SNOWPATCH SPIRE

Deus ex Machina
VI 5.9/A2
Photo on p. 111
Protection:
    2 sets Friends to #4, extra to 6″
    2 sets wires, 1 set RPs
    2 sets TCUs to #3
    4 KB
    12 LA

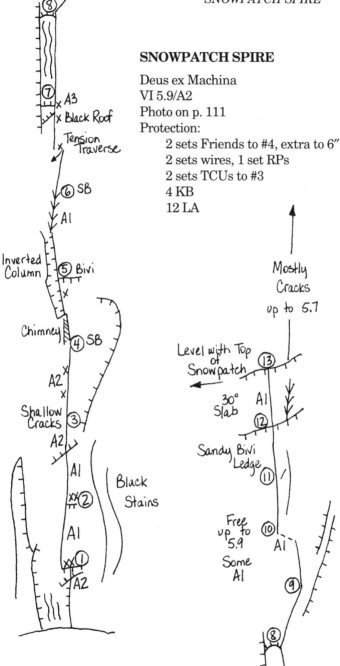

Fig. 37. *Snowpatch Spire, Deus ex Machina*

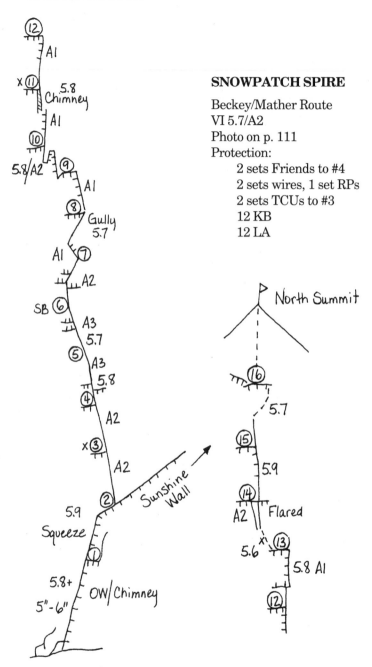

SNOWPATCH SPIRE

Beckey/Mather Route
VI 5.7/A2
Photo on p. 111
Protection:
  2 sets Friends to #4
  2 sets wires, 1 set RPs
  2 sets TCUs to #3
  12 KB
  12 LA

Fig. 38. *Snowpatch Spire, Beckey-Mather Route*

II In Harm's Way

VI   5.8/A4 *(photo, p. 111)*

Left (south) of Deus ex Machina/Sunshine Wall, start in obvious crack system that ascends directly to N Summit. This route is independent, except for about the last three pitches where it joins Deus ex Machina. Further details unavailable. *Time:* 3 days. *Descent:* Beckey-Greenwood Route, W Face.

JJ East Face Diagonal

VI   5.7/A3 *(photo, p. 111)*

Route starts about 100 feet south of Deus ex Machina/Sunshine Wall and follows obvious diagonal crack line through lower half of face, then corner systems to N Summit. Few details are available. Nail dirt and moss-filled crack until several pitches beyond overhangs where crack intersects large open book. Mostly free-climbing on upper face to summit. *Time:* 2–3 days. *Descent:* Rappel Beckey-Greenwood Route, W Face.

KK Beckey-Mather Route

VI   5.7/A2 *(fig. 38) (photo, p. 111)*

Direct line to S Summit; route starts 300 feet north of big corner in face below right edge of prominent snowpatch. A large, white, hanging column marks the cracks on lower face. **1–4** Aid cracks to tip of column (crux). **5–8** Chimney to right edge of column and aid to ledge; follow crack to tension traverse and aid thin crack through black roofs (second crux). **9–12** Angle of face is lower, but climbing above is strenuous with some aid to sandy bivi ledge. **13+** Aid crack up slab till level with top of snowpatch, then follow broken ground, mostly cracks (5.7) up to S Summit. *Time:* 2–3 days. *Descent:* Rappel Kraus-McCarthy Route, W Face.

PIGEON SPIRE
10,250 ft. (3124 m)

Appearance and Location

When viewed from the upper Vowell Glacier, this striking spire resembles the profile of a pigeon preparing for takeoff from its lofty perch. The spire's ridge crest divides the north end of the Bugaboo Glacier and the south end of the Vowell Glacier in an east-west line.

The pigeon's immense granite breast, formed in part by the sweeping slab of the lower east face, faces east toward Snowpatch Spire. Its neck, head, and beak are thrust upwards, creating a dramatic pointed summit. Pigeon's left wing forms a slight arete or buttress that sweeps from the Vowell Glacier to the summit—a feature that is especially noticeable at sunset and sunrise. The glaciers have receded enough to reveal one of the bird's toes (Pigeontoe) on the lower northeast side of the E Face slab. Its back, a steep-sided ridge, gradually descends from the beak/summit to its tail. The pigeon's tail feathers extend into the depression of the east side of the Pigeon-Howser Col.

When viewed from the east, Pigeon appears to be completely detached and surrounded by ice. When viewed from the west, however, it is seen as part of a vast cirque that extends south in a seemingly continuous sweeping wall of steep granite.

Notable First Ascents

Pigeon was first climbed during the summer of 1930 when Peter Kaufmann, one of Kain's fellow guides, led Eaton Cromwell to its summit via the now-classic W Ridge. They scouted the easiest line to the summit and, in keeping with the true spirit of early mountaineering, Kaufmann led the entire climb without protection. He used the rope only to assist his client up the steep steps near the summit. Today, this route has a Class 5 rating of 5.4, although many modern mountaineers still climb it in the same traditional style as Kaufmann and Cromwell, Class 4.

Climbing Pigeon Spire

Considered today to be one of the showcase climbs of the Bugaboos, the W Ridge route on Pigeon is an excellent way to become acquainted with alpine rock climbing, Bugaboo style.

Although Pigeon is relatively close to the hut, the shortest approach involves negotiating a sometimes dangerous col (pass) that separates the Crescent and Vowell glaciers. This col, known as the Bugaboo-Snowpatch Col, has an ever-widening bergschrund that splits the entire snowface on its east side. Several accidents and a death have occurred here because of bad timing and inexperience.

Crevasse danger exists on the Crescent and Vowell glaciers, and avalanche and rockfall danger are always present on the east side of the col. It is wise to plan your approach to Pigeon so you can climb or descend the col early or late in the day when the snow is firm and the rocks are frozen in place.

The uphill approach to Pigeon Spire via the Bugaboo-Snowpatch Col takes 1.5 to 3 hours depending on your pace. If you are inexperienced with the terrain in the Bugaboos, give yourself plenty of extra time to get to the spires—that means leave the hut early!

Although Pigeon's granite is often covered with lichen, it is generally very rough and solid. As a result, it is excellent for friction climbing and for placing bombproof protection. Routes on Pigeon vary in difficulty from the easiest, W Ridge (II 5.4), to more challenging routes like Cleopatra's Alley (IV 5.10 A2). The most common descent, for all routes, is to down-climb the W Ridge; no fixed rappel stations exist. Allow plenty of time to return to the hut via the col.

Route Descriptions

A   West Ridge

II   5.4 *(photo, p. 122)*

Approach: Ascend upper Vowell Glacier to Pigeon-Howser Col. Follow easy snow gully to notch on ridge proper near west end. Scramble up to SW Summit (false) via easy friction slabs. Down-climb to notch and climb up to second false summit. Step right and down-climb a narrow chimney or jam crack to sloping ledges on northwest side. Alternately, step left, follow ledge system that descends to same sloping ledges on northwest side. Traverse east and follow line of least resistance until it is possible to follow hand and finger cracks to summit gully. Scramble gully/ledge system to summit blocks. *Time:* 1.5–2 hours from Pigeon-Howser Col to summit. *Descent:* Down-climb same route.

B   Tail-feather Pinnacle-Right Side

II   5.10– *(fig. 39) (photo, p. 122)*

Approach: Same as for W Ridge. Cross bergschrund and gain right side of black pinnacle formed by stacked flakes that point to notch east of SW Summit. **1** Jam, lieback, and chimney flakes and blocks in main corner until it is possible to move left. **2–3** Jam steep hand crack (crux) to blocky ledge belay; continue past blocks to gain upper (main) face of pinnacle. Easy face climbing leads to large ledge belay at top of pinnacle. **4** Traverse right 20 feet on small ledge to gain vertical quartz dike. Face-climb dike (no protection) to W Ridge skyline near large V-notch. A direct variation up corner proper is possible (5.10 +), with finish on dike pitch. *Time:* 3–4 hours from bergschrund to summit. *Descent:* Down-climb W Ridge.

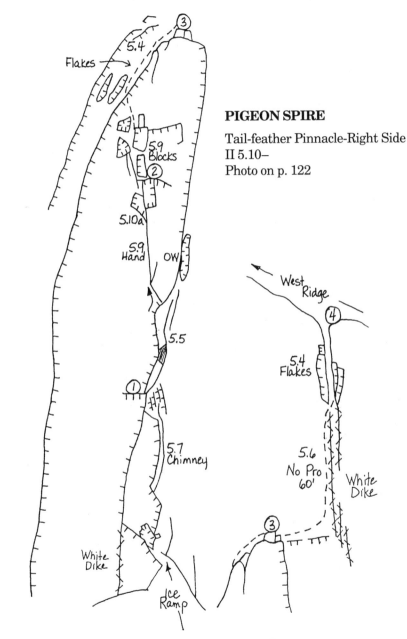

PIGEON SPIRE

Tail-feather Pinnacle-Right Side
II 5.10–
Photo on p. 122

Fig. 39. *Pigeon Spire, Tail-feather Pinnacle*
Photo: *Pigeon Spire, N Face*

C   Feather Fallout

III   5.7/A2 *(photo, p. 122)*

Approach: Same as for W Ridge. Route starts several hundred feet left of Tail-feather Pinnacle. Directly below the right edge of the large snowfield on upper N Face, a crack system leading straight up to about two-thirds height of face begins in a small inconspicuous open book. 1 Aid and free-climb thin crack (70 feet). Belay at end of short rotten gully. 2 Follow dihedral formed by flakes (40 feet). Aid steep crack 60 feet to small belay ledge. 3 Mixed free and aid moves (40 feet) lead to cave belay. 4 Climb left out of cave a few feet until it is possible to scramble to base of right-slanting chimney. Chimney to large scree-covered ledge for belay. 5 Climb rotten left-facing dihedral to the right of belay ledge (80 feet), then scramble to top of gully, belay. 6 Follow gully system to W Ridge. Follow W Ridge to summit. **Time:** 6–7 hours from bergschrund to summit. **Descent:** Down-climb W Ridge.

D   Northwest Face

III   5.7/A3 *(photo, p. 122)*

Approach: Same as for W Ridge. This route ascends a plumb line to the summit. The line is several hundred feet east of Tail-feather Pinnacle. 1–2 Cross bergschrund aid right-slanting thin aid crack. 3 Aid-climb long pitch past bulge. 4 Lieback to right-sloping ledge. Move left and free-climb vertical open book with abundant holds. 5–6 Free-climb easier ground to snowfield. 7 Climb one pitch of snow/ice to gain easy slabs to summit. **Time:** 4–6 hours from bergschrund to summit. **Descent:** Down-climb W Ridge.

E   Wingtip

III   5.10– *(fig. 40) (photos, pp. 122, 127)*

Approach: Same as for W Ridge. This elegant line follows the crest of the pigeon's left wing. Line is highlighted at sunrise and sunset by sun and shadow. After crossing bergschrund, 1 ascend a steep right-facing corner (crux) with a widening crack to an alcove. Step right and follow flakes to crest of arete and spacious ledge. 2 Climb hand crack that widens to chimney, belay at top of large flakes. 3 Climb 40-degree slab split by easy cracks to roof. Skirt roof to left and belay at horn. 4 Follow second slab to four-foot roof. Move left and climb to dramatic, sloping outside corner. 5 Shinny sharp arete ("bareback pitch"), no protection, to roomy ledge below blocky buttress, above snowfield. Follow NW Face to

PIGEON SPIRE

Wingtip
III 5.10–
Photos on pp. 122, 127
Protection:
    Standard rack to 4″
    Extra to 6″

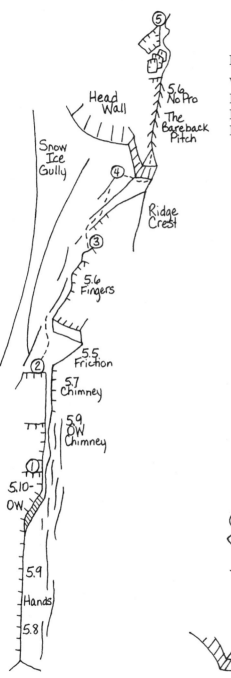

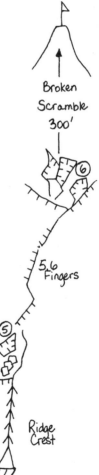

Fig. 40. *Pigeon Spire, Wingtip*

summit. *Time:* 3–4 hours from bergschrund to summit. *Descent:* Down-climb W Ridge.

F   North Face

IV   5.7/A2 *(photos, pp. 122, 127)*

Approach: Same as for Wingtip. On the east side of the N Face, a prominent break or couloir splits the wall to the shoulder formed by the meeting of the E and N faces; following this line is truly a mixed alpine experience. Cross bergschrund. **1–2** Climb 50-degree ice/snow (300 feet), belay on left side. **3** Aid thin cracks on right wall to roof, often wet. **4** Aid through wet overhang to gain ice patch. **5–6** Cross ice moving left (300 feet) to gain upper 70-degree black, lichen-covered slab. **7** Follow 2-inch crack to step on shoulder of N Ridge. At ice patch, traverse right and join Wingtip to summit. *Time:* 7–8 hours from bergschrund to summit. *Descent:* Down-climb W Ridge.

G   Variation: Northeast Ridge/Miller-Shepard Route

5.6 *(photos, pp. 122, 127)*

Approach: Same as for Wingtip. Scramble to start at Pigeontoe-notch. **1** Climb white wall and **2** blocky section to small slab left of N Face couloir. The smaller sloping slab parallels the major E Face slab, but much lower. **3** Climb steep blocky section to gain ridge. **4–5** Follow ridge proper to snowfield (may be icy). **6** Continue up cracks and slabs (5.6) to join original route on ridge to avoid ice in couloir. *Time:* 4 hours from bergschrund to summit. *Descent:* Down-climb W Ridge.

EAST AND SOUTH FACES

(photos, pp. 127, 131)

Approaches for routes on Pigeon's E and S faces may be easiest by ascending the Bugaboo Glacier. From Kain Hut, scramble moraine ridges on north side of glacier until it is possible to skirt south around the lowest rampart of Snowpatch's SE Corner. Continue south of Snowpatch across glacier. Crevasse danger exists and conditions change from year to year, depending on winter snow accumulations. Use caution, especially late in season. Alternate approach to S slopes via Bugaboo-Snowpatch Col and by crossing the lowest point on W Ridge.

H   East Face

V   5.7/A1 or 5.10– *(fig. 41) (photo, p. 127)*

Approach: Via the Bugaboo Glacier by traversing around the south end of Snowpatch Spire to avoid the dangerous icefall in

Pigeon Spire, E Face

PIGEON SPIRE

E Face
IV 5.7/A1 (5.10–)
Photo on p. 127
Protection:
    2 sets Friends to #4
    1 set wires
    1 set TCUs to #3

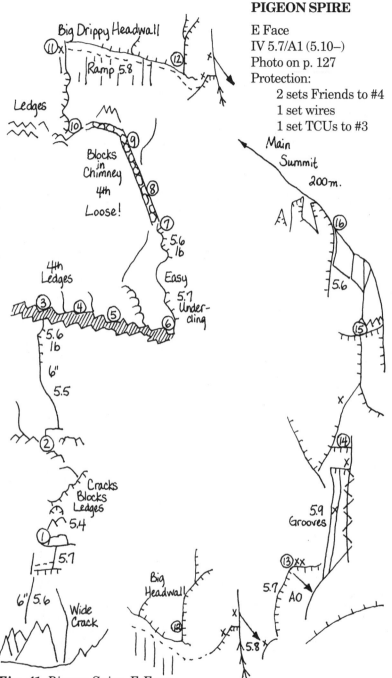

Fig. 41. *Pigeon Spire, E Face*

Pigeon-Snowpatch Col. Layton Kor and Ed Cooper called this route a potential classic. It is, in dry conditions. However, snowmelt from the upper snowslopes drains onto the tricky friction pitches at the top of the slab. Aid (tension traverse) is used to pass this section. At the lowest point of the south (left) side of the enormous 60-degree slab, **1–3** ascend cracks and a chimney until it is possible to gain access to ledge that traverses face. **4–6** Move right to its end. **7–10** Climb cracks to gain another chimney/gully that ascends leftward along the upper slab. At end of gully, **11** climb cracks to base of headwall. **12–13** Friction right and up flakes to left-facing corner. **14** Climb grooves, flakes, and slabs to ridge crest. Finish via N Ridge. *Time:* 8–9 hours from bergschrund to summit. ***Descent:*** Down-climb W Ridge.

I   Cleopatra's Alley

V   5.10/A2 *(fig. 42) (photo, p. 127)*

Approach: Same as E Face. Scramble past blocks to crack system on south side of main slab. **1–5** Follow easy cracks to base of headwall. **6** Follow arching left-facing flake cracks to another low-angle slab. Move left to gain ledge at base of right-leaning crack. **7** Climb short, steep cracks to the right (broken by small ledges) to upper low-angle slab with snow. **8** Move left past blank wall and overhanging chimney to alcove with block. **9** Climb the steep finger cracks to a ledge. **10** Ascend easy cracks to ledge (wall behind is split by two short offwidths). Wrestle with driest offwidth to large ledge above. **11–12** Scramble up and left to final finger cracks that lead to summit. ***Time:*** 12–13 hours from bergschrund to summit. ***Descent:*** Down-climb W Ridge.

J   Southeast Buttress

V   5.8/A2 *(photos, pp. 127, 131)*

Approach: Same as for E Face. Buttress lies between slabby E and S faces. Line follows an obvious corner on the upper face. Scramble gullies and slabs to gain access to the huge, sloping ramp that descends the S Face from west to east. **1** Climb inside corner system, mostly aid through overhangs to hanging belay. **2** Aid through an overhang and follow a flaky crack to ledge 300 feet above the "Great Ledge." **3** Move right, climb cracks (mostly aid) to a 2-foot ledge. **4** Climb solitary crack up blank wall. **5–7** Climb short pitches on steep ground (some aid). **8–10** Moderate climbing to short step **11** below summit block. ***Time:*** 1.5 days from glacier. ***Descent:*** Down-climb W Ridge.

PIGEON SPIRE

Cleopatra's Alley
IV 5.10/A2
Photo on p. 127
Protection:
  2 sets Friends to #4
  2 sets wires
  Extra to 7"

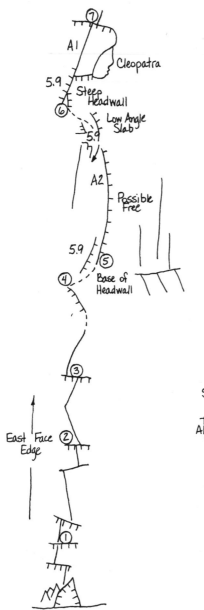
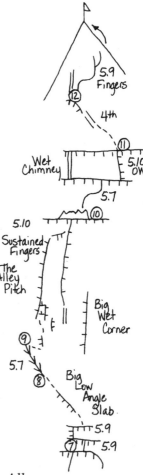

Fig. 42. *Pigeon Spire, Cleopatra's Alley*
Photo: *Pigeon Spire, S Face*

K Southeast Buttress Variation

III 5.6 *(photo, p. 131)*

Approach: Route begins and ascends same crack systems as for Cleopatra's Alley. At top of slab, rappel to Great Ledge and scramble to where it joins W Ridge. *Time:* 4–5 hours. *Descent:* Down-climb W Ridge.

L South Face

III 5.6/A1 *(photo, p. 131)*

Approach: Same as for E Face. Gain access to Great Ledge via a drainage gully. Once on ramp, route follows obvious large dihedral to notch west of summit. Aid 90-foot overhanging crack to gain access to dihedral. Account is unclear, but climbing above was mostly free. *Time:* 5–6 hours. *Descent:* Down-climb W Ridge.

M Parboosing Route

III 5.5 *(fig. 43)*

Approach: Same as for E Face or W Ridge. Route follows line of least resistance, on the west end of the S Face, from large silver slab with numerous cracks to the first false summit on W Ridge. Protection is marginal on upper pitches, but belay stances are good. **1–2** Ascend water crack system up and left to just below a roof. **3** Traverse right under roof, then climb up and right to small ledge. **4** Climb up and left across wet area to belay stance near dihedral system. **5–6** Move left past corner and climb two superb parallel cracks (vertical), then face-climb crystals to easy friction slab above. Scramble (Class 3) up and left along ridge and exit right to first false summit on W Ridge. Continue on to summit via W Ridge. *Time:* 4–5 hours from base to summit. *Descent:* Down-climb W Ridge.

N Lambice Tour

II 5.8 *(fig. 43)*

Approach: Same as for Parboosing Route. The route follows obvious chimney system on S Face to slabs of first false summit on W Ridge. Start 1000 feet east of the W Ridge saddle. **1** Face-climb up and right to block in chimney. **2** Move right out of chimney and follow flakes to bolt below roof. **3** Climb through roof (crux) to gain easy slabs to false summit on W Ridge. Continue on to summit via W Ridge Route. *Time:* 2–3 hours from base to summit. *Descent:* Down-climb W Ridge.

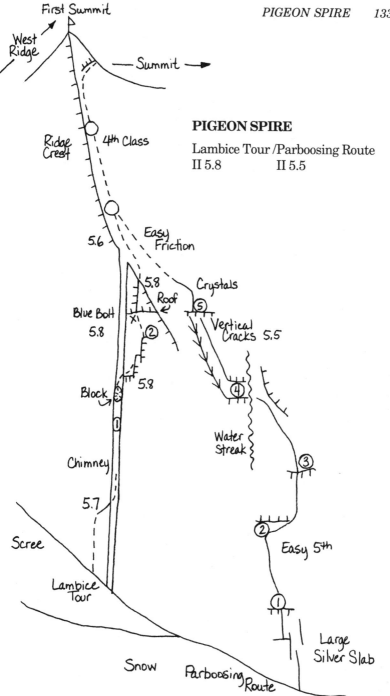

First Summit

West Ridge

Summit →

Ridge Crest

4th Class

PIGEON SPIRE

Lambice Tour / Parboosing Route
II 5.8   II 5.5

5.6

Easy Friction

5.8

Roof

Crystals

Blue Bolt
5.8

X

② Vertical Cracks 5.5

Block

5.8

①

④

Chimney

Water Streak

5.7

③

Scree

②

Easy 5th

Lambice Tour

①

Large Silver Slab

Snow   Parboosing Route

Fig. 43. *Pigeon Spire, Parboosing Route and Lambice Tour*

PIGEONTOE

West Summit

II   5.3–5.4 *(photo, p. 122)*

On the lower east side of the N Face is a tower that is separated from the main face by a deep notch. The two summit pinnacles look like up-turned toes of Pigeon's northeast foot. **Approach:** Same as for N Face. Ascend the couloir to the prominent notch (Pigeon-Pigeontoe notch). **1–3** Climb cracks and slabs to sharp W summit. **Time:** 2 hours from notch. **Descent:** Rappel same route.

PIGEONFEATHERS

9650 ft. (2941 m)

Appearance and Location

These peaks are three distinct summits, part of a ridge that extends south from Pigeon Spire's W Ridge. They seem minor when viewed from the upper Bugaboo Glacier, because the neve extends nearly to their summits. When viewed from the E Creek Basin, however, they present themselves as an interesting series of steep towers, turrets, and faces.

Like many of the peaks and spires in the Bugaboo Group, they are aligned in a northwest-southeast direction, but their faces and ridges have been named after the main compass coordinates.

The W Peak's summit (closest to Pigeon Spire) is but a mere rise in the main ridge-line, but its adjoining SW Tower stands sentinellike, 800 to 900 feet above the snows on the E Creek side near the Pigeon-Howser Col. A 45-degree snowfield extends from its base toward the deep notch northwest of the central or E Peak (so named in the Kruszyna-Putnam guide).

The E Peak is the highest of the group. As with the W Peak, the upper Bugaboo Glacier extends close to its rocky summit. Its SW Face drops sharply into the East Creek Basin, however. Larger and more complex, the E Peak has two ridges that extend from the main summit ridge to the southwest. These ridges embrace a snowfield that extends from the basin to the bottom of the steep 900-foot W Face of the peak. The summit ridge curves gently southeast to a deep notch that separates the E and SE peaks. A

Pigeonfeathers, W Face

Pigeon

Snowpatch

E Peak

SE Peak

W Peak

E Creek Basin

prominent Y-shaped couloir extends from the notch to the E Creek Basin.

Towerlike in appearance when viewed from the E Creek Basin, the SE Peak appears as a small bump when seen from the Bugaboo Glacier, because the neve extends to its summit. But on the southwest side, a long, elegant arete rises to its flat summit. Adjacent to this arete, a narrow and near-vertical W Face dominates this view of the peak.

Notable First Ascents

The routes are generally snow/ice walk-ups or easy climbing.

Climbing Pigeonfeathers

It would be a mistake to discourage climbers from venturing onto the untouched SW faces and ridge-lines of these peaks but as this is written, only the summits have been explored.

The rock is of high quality and the features on this side offer aesthetic and elegant crack lines. It is a mystery why no one has explored them more extensively. The main reason why so few routes exist probably relates to their proximity to Pigeon and the Howsers. These spires are immensely popular and draw the majority of Bugaboo climbers, leaving Pigeonfeathers alone and unexplored.

It is best to approach Pigeonfeathers via the Bugaboo-Snowpatch Col and the Vowell Glacier to the Pigeon-Howser Col or the W Ridge of Pigeon. However, it is possible to reach the summits by ascending the north fork of the Bugaboo Glacier from Kain Hut. Descents are short down-climbs and walk-offs to the upper Bugaboo Glacier or down the couloirs and gullies between the peaks on their western flanks.

Route Descriptions

A   West Peak

II   5.3–5.4 *(photo, p. 135)*

Approach: Gain upper Bugaboo Glacier via north fork approach or by descending from low point on Pigeon's W Ridge along snow-ridge. Make descending traverse from Bugaboo Neve across NW Flank of E Peak to notch. Traverse out on narrow ledges above sheer E Face, then to summit. Short, exposed finger traverse is key to ascent. ***Time:*** 1 hour from neve. ***Descent:*** Down-climb same route.

B East Peak

II *(photo, p. 135)*

Approach: From upper Bugaboo Neve to east side of peak. Ascend snowslope to summit. *Time:* 1 hour or less. *Descent:* Down-climb same route.

HOWSER SPIRE MASSIF
11,150 ft. (3398 m)

Appearance and Location

The three towers of the Howser Massif (referred to collectively as Howser Spire) define the western limit of the Bugaboo Group. Called the N, Central, and S towers, the peaks actually align in a true northwest-southeast configuration.

The view of Howser Spire from the east—as seen from the Vowell Glacier or the summits of Bugaboo, Snowpatch, or Pigeon—is more striking for its alpine aspect than its quantity of steep granite. Three distinct summits emerge from the Vowell Glacier. The N Tower, tallest and most complex of the three, terminates in a long, broken ridge that runs north toward the lower Vowell Glacier. This long ridge is bisected by a prominent east-west spur ridge, which breaks the tower into distinct snow-plastered E and NE faces.

From the north, this appearance of a long N Ridge is revealed actually as a triangular, low-angle N Face, with ridge-lines to the east and west. The NW Ridge provides access to the long and difficult routes on the west side of the N Tower.

Viewed from the west—as seen from the air above the E Creek Basin (photo, p. 141)—Howser presents a dramatic spectacle of long, sweeping buttresses and sheer granite walls. E Creek Basin is considerably lower than the Vowell Glacier; hence, the tremendous increase in the apparent height of all the towers when seen from the west.

The W Face of the N Tower is truly awesome—nearly vertical and 3000 feet from base to summit. The Central Tower has the least impressive W Face of the three. It is approximately half the height of the N and S towers, since its lower portion is dominated by a massive snowfield. The W Face of the S Tower is nearly as grand as that of the N Tower, and it is characterized by a long, prominent buttress ascending from foot to summit.

Farther to the south, the Minaret is an appendant feature of the SW Face of the S Tower. It is really a separate tower, lower than the S Tower by some 800 feet, but endowed with long vertical faces on three sides.

Notable First Ascents

When Conrad Kain led the MacCarthys, the Vincents, and Henry Frind to the summit of the N Tower, in August 1916, climbing was inaugurated in the Bugaboos.

It was not until 1941 that the summit of the S Tower was reached. Lloyd Anderson (founder of Recreational Equipment, Inc.), Helmey Beckey (Fred Beckey's younger brother), L. Boyer, and T. Campbell ascended the mixed alpine route now called the E Face-Ridge.

The Central Tower was last of the individual summits to be ascended. During the summer of 1955, G. Austin, D. Bernays, James McCarthy, and John Rupley successfully climbed the N Ridge.

During the summer of 1961, Fred Beckey and Yvon Chouinard made the first ascent of the huge W Buttress on the S Tower, a climb considered equal to the long granite climbs of the West Alps. This kicked off the pursuit of hard routes on the west side of Howser, activity that included the 1971 ascent of the W Face of the N Tower by Galen Rowell, Chris Jones, and Tony Quamar. The following decade saw several new Grade VIs established on the N Tower, as well as activity on the S Tower Minaret.

Climbing Howser Spire

While Snowpatch Spire offers the highest concentration of established routes in the Bugaboos, Howser Spire presents the greatest opportunity for pioneering new routes of high standard and the most potential for the true "big mountain" experience.

Negotiating the upper Vowell Glacier dissuades most visitors from attempting even the easier climbs on the eastern ridges and faces. Some of these climbs, such as the E Face of the N Tower, are as close to mixed alpine routes as can be found in the Bugaboos. Even the pure rock climbs from the east require a certain degree of mountain experience on the approach.

All visits to the western reaches of Howser are serious ventures, demanding top physical condition and high technical skills. The W Buttress Route (Beckey-Chouinard) on the S Tower is perhaps the most sought-after climb in the Bugaboos. At Grade V 5.10, and requiring no aid climbing, it is also probably the *easiest* established route on the west side of Howser. Most of the routes

East faces of South and Central Howser towers

on the western faces and buttresses are Grade VI, and even the Grade Vs require aid-climbing technique.

The climbs on the west side of Howser are among the most difficult rock climbs in Canada; if these do not present enough challenge, then choose your own line. When something new is done on the Howsers, it is generally the highlight of the climbing season in the Bugaboos. As this is written, even the Minaret on the S Tower has yet to go totally free—with but a few aid moves remaining, that should be solved soon. At present, there are no routes on the W Face of the Central Tower. Discontinuous cracks and down-sloping slabs present the chief obstacles. A dark, wet chimney appears to be the only uninterrupted weakness on the face, although it may be more reasonable to attempt in winter conditions.

If the dream of a climbing hut somewhere at the base of the west side of Howser is ever realized, some of the logistical impediments to the tremendous W Face climbs will be removed. For now, climbs of the Howsers from the west require more planning and more effort than most casual visitors to the Bugaboos care to expend. But for the truly adventuresome, and for climbers looking for the ultimate in difficult alpine rock climbs, look to the lofty western buttresses of the Howser Towers.

The approach to the Howsers is best via the Bugaboo-Snowpatch Col and across the upper Vowell Glacier. Routes on the west side of the S Tower can be reached via the Pigeon-Howser Col. Routes on the west side of the N Tower are easier to approach by skirting the Howsers to the north, across the NW Ridge.

Descents are generally all by rappel down the E faces of each tower. Anchors are fairly obvious and usually follow direct lines from the summits to the bergschrund, which sometimes requires an additional rappel to cross. It is possible to down-climb the E Face-S Ridge and E Face-N Ridge routes (N Tower). It is possible to down-climb the N Ridge Route (Central Tower); however, the rappel routes are preferred. The Central and N towers are climbed less often, so anchor slings may need to be replaced.

Route Descriptions

Routes are listed in a counterclockwise fashion, starting with the E Face of each tower.

NORTH TOWER

Approach: For routes on the E Face, go from the Pigeon-Howser Col, traverse northwest under the E faces of the S and

Howser Spire Massif, E Face

Central towers (about 2 hours from Kain Hut). Crevasse danger is always present on the upper Vowell Glacier; roped glacier travel is recommended. ***Descent:*** Scramble down N Ridge to small gendarme or "fang" that protrudes out over E Face (just below ridge north of summit); rappel once (160 feet) from fang, to snow/ice slopes (mid E Face). Down-climb and rappel over bergschrund.

A   East Face-South Ridge

II   Class 4 *(photo, p. 141)*

The route ascends steep snowslopes and slabby rock above the bergschrund to the notch between the Central and N Towers, then follows the S Ridge to main summit. Cross bergschrund and climb snow (50 degrees) to broken rock ledges/slabs; work left to gain notch on ridge. Climb ridge, detour right (onto E Face) to avoid blank slabs. One rope length below the summit, traverse through a window behind huge block that caps a rib; scramble to summit. ***Time:*** 4–5 hours from bergschrund. ***Descent:*** Rappel E Face or down-climb same route.

B   East Face-North Ridge

III   5.4 *(photo, p. 141)*

The intersection of E and N ridges forms a bay that marks the start of this route, which ascends to broken rock and N Ridge crest to summit. From bergschrund, climb steep snow to rock and follow shallow couloir to low point on N Ridge (between E Ridge gendarme and N Tower summit). Climb ridge to final slabs below summit (E Face). Traverse slabs to projecting knob and cross narrow chimney to far side. Ascend steep slabs to summit. ***Time:*** 6–7 hours from base. ***Descent:*** Rappel E Face or down-climb same route.

C   East Ridge-North Ridge

III   5.4 *(photo, p. 141)*

This route starts in the same general area as E Face-N Ridge Route, but continues north and up snow to the E Ridge crest. Once on E Ridge, follow corniced ridge crest to base of prominent dark gendarme on N Ridge-E Ridge intersection. Move left (south) and climb two short pitches (Class 5) followed by snow-covered ledges and chimneys to main N Ridge (south of gendarme). Continue along N Ridge to summit. ***Time:*** 6–7 hours from bergschrund. ***Descent:*** Rappel E Face.

Howser Spire Massif, NW Face (access couloir marked by arrow)

S Tower

N Tower

D

E/F

E

F

G

H

J

D   North Ridge Integral

III   5.4 *(photo, p. 141)*

Approach: From the Bugaboo-Snowpatch Col, descend the Vowell Glacier until it is possible to avoid icefall and gain snowslopes at toe of N Ridge (3 hours from Kain Hut). This fine route traverses the entire N Ridge. Ascend easy snowslopes on west side several hundred feet, then climb short Class 5 lead to regain ridge crest proper. Exposed but moderate climbing to top of gendarme-E Ridge intersection. Descend gully to saddle and join E Ridge-N Ridge Route to summit. ***Time:*** 6–7 hours from base. ***Descent:*** Rappel E Face.

E   Northwest Face

V   5.8/A2 *(photo, p. 143)*

Approach: Same as for N Ridge Integral, then continue southwest across a pass (8400 feet) to lower flanks of N Face and notch/saddle (9100 feet) in NW Ridge. From the notch, descend a gully toward the southwest to base of NW Face (see photo); alternate approach is to descend from Bill's Pass toward Juniper Lake and traverse around toe of NW Ridge to base of NW Face. Route takes line of least resistance up a sickle-shaped ledge, then around the right side of two snowfields enclosed by the N-NW Ridge and W Buttress, finishing on 600-foot headwall above. **1–5** Moderate climbing (5.6) to snow "finger" that descends from lower snowfield. Ascend right side of snowfield and climb short wall that leads to upper snowfield. Again, ascend right side of snowfield to directly below summit. Traverse ice right, climb crack system on buttress (mixed ground, ice/rock four pitches) to ledge under huge roof; aid around and climb three more pitches on wall to summit ridge. Exact details unclear, bivouac spot below summit is adequate. Considerable objective hazards from rock/icefall on upper face. ***Time:*** 1–2 days. ***Descent:*** Rappel E Face.

F   West Buttress

V   5.7/A2 *(photos, pp. 143, 145)*

Approach: Same as for NW Face. Traverse toe of W Buttress and ascend small glacier to base of W Face. Buttress rises in two giant steps with a narrow snow couloir separating it from the main W Face. Route follows couloir to top of first step and ascends next step to gain upper snowfield and join NW Route. Ascend couloir

Howser Spire Massif, W Face (access couloir marked by arrow)

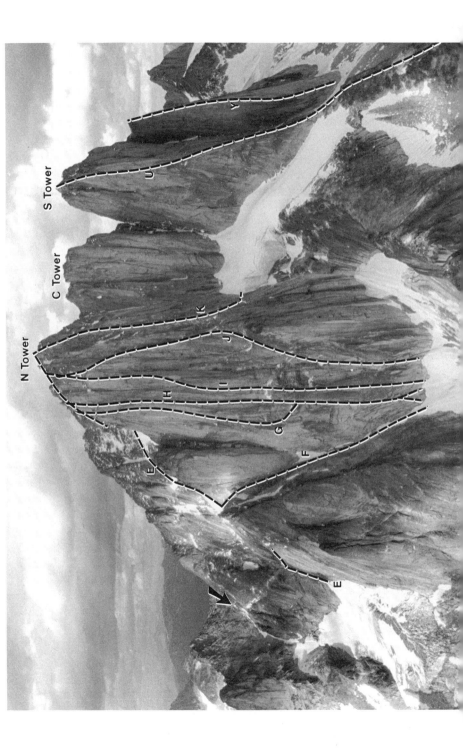

past lower slabs to top of first step (snow, then rock). Climb main buttress to top of second step (some aid on wet rock). Rappel onto hanging upper snowfield on NW Face (awkward). Join NW Face Route to summit. *Time:* 2 days. *Descent:* Rappel E Face.

G All Along the Watchtower

VI   5.10/A2 *(fig. 44) (photos, pp. 143, 145)*

Approach: Same as for W Buttress. This is a major variant of Warrior. Route follows Warrior for the first nine pitches (slabby), then works left and follows obvious left-facing corner capped by roofs on left side of W Face to summit ridge. Eventually, it joins NW Face-W Buttress Route to finish. **1–9** Ascend Warrior to broken ledge area (good-quality free climbing to 5.10). **10–13** Climb diagonally left to gain steep corner system and ledge (good bivi). **14–24** Work right on easy ground to gain corner system (easy aid in shallow, thin finger-size cracks in good rock, could possibly go free). Follow to terraces. **21–24** Scramble and climb moderately easy ground to summit ridge. *Time:* 3–4 days. *Descent:* Rappel E Face.

H West Face-Left/Warrior

VI   5.9/A3 *(fig. 45) (photos, pp. 143, 145)*

Approach: Same as for W Buttress. This climb starts right of the W Buttress gully, but left of the main W Face gully system that leads directly to the summit. Route follows a direct line to the summit ridge just north of the summit. **1–5** Climb obvious crack/chimney system (good ledges at top of pitches 3 and 5). **6–9** Climb steep wall through roofs to broken ground (fair bivi site). **10–11** Work up and right to gain single crack system. **12–18** Pass roofs to top of pillar (good bivi). **19–20** Climb to ridge crest and join NW Face-W Buttress Route to summit. *Time:* 3–4 days. *Descent:* Rappel E Face.

I Mescalito

VI   5.9/A3 *(photos, pp. 143, 145)*

Approach: Same as for W Buttress. Route parallels Warrior for a couple hundred feet right (south), eventually joining Seventh Rifle near summit. **1–10** Climb to gain two large cracks that eventually lead to base of steep wall (mostly free). Climb up, then right to long straight-in crack through roof. Move left (hard aid) to obvious right-facing corner to top of big tower (good bivi). Climb right from tower to good crack, ledge. Move left and climb one pitch to ridge crest and top. Most aid is A1 with occasional A3. Further details unclear. *Time:* 3–4 days. *Descent:* Rappel E Face.

HOWSER SPIRE

North Tower

All Along the Watchtower
VI 5.10/A2
Photos on pp. 143, 145
Protection:
  2 sets Friends to #4
  2 sets TCUs to #3
  2 sets wires, extra RPs
  2 KB
  2 LA

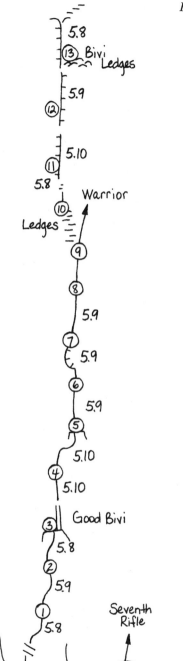

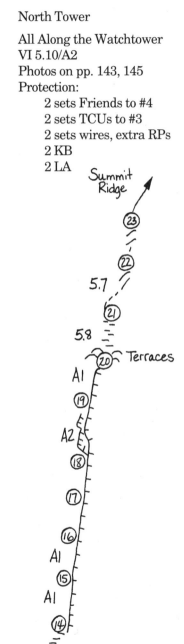

Fig. 44. *Howser Spire, All Along the Watchtower*

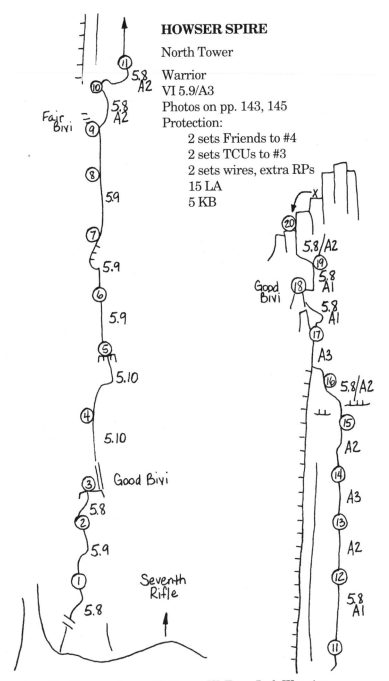

HOWSER SPIRE

North Tower

Warrior
VI 5.9/A3
Photos on pp. 143, 145
Protection:
2 sets Friends to #4
2 sets TCUs to #3
2 sets wires, extra RPs
15 LA
5 KB

Fig. 45. Howser Spire, N Tower W Face-Left Warrior

J West Face-Right/Seventh Rifle

VI 5.9/A2 or 5.11/A1 *(photos, pp. 143, 145)*

Approach: Same as for W Buttress. Route starts several hundred feet right of Mescalito and angles right to gain crest of central buttress on W Face to notch in ridge crest north of summit. Near lowest point of face, climb two short crack pitches to prominent gully (5.10 and 5.9). Climb eight to nine pitches that angle slightly right to terraces, looking for easy way (5.8 corner followed by face climbing to terrace) to big ledge on top of lower buttress (good bivi). At south end of ledge, climb cracks to gain another gully system (four to six pitches); stay inside gully on left to large wet chimney, then move outside to gain clean cracks (four to five pitches to broken corner). Step out left into broken corner system (some rotten rock, many 5.8 pitches) to exit cracks. Ascend exit cracks for three pitches (groove with roof) until angle eases; climb two more pitches to ridge. Easy Class 5 and Class 4 (four pitches) along ridge to summit. 34 pitches in all, a worthwhile modern route that goes free except for a few points of aid. ***Time:*** 2–3 days. ***Descent:*** Rappel E Face.

K Southwest Face

V 5.7/A2 *(photos, pp. 145, 154)*

Approach: Same as for Beckey-Chouinard Route on S Tower. Scramble the first 1000 feet of the buttress at the foot of the W Face of S Tower to gain hanging glacier at the base of the W Face of Central Tower. Where this small glacier meets the steep rock rampart that drops toward the base of the N Tower's W Face, there is an excellent bivi site under a large boulder. (First ascent party used this site for their base camp.) From the hanging glacier, the route ascends a gully system to the summit. Step onto an obvious "gangway" off glacier and climb to pinnacle at its end. Rappel diagonally left to gain crack system; climb 200 feet to large ledge. Cross corner up and right; aid short wall (250 feet; A2). Climb dihedral and couloir system over roofs (left) at top of wall. Continue climbing mixed rock/ice for 800 feet to final wall; climb chimney in center to easier ground below summit. ***Time:*** 1–2 days. ***Descent:*** Rappel E Face.

CENTRAL TOWER

Approach: For the E Face, same as for the N Tower.

L North Ridge

III *(photo, p. 141)*

This route follows steep snow/ice on the E Face to Central-N Tower Col. Generally a line of least resistance, once on rock ridge a steep, rotten and difficult chimney (Class 5) on east side must be surmounted to gain the summit. The Class 5 rating is debatable depending on the strength and experience of the party. *Time:* 3–4 hours from bergschrund. *Descent:* Down-climb and rappel same route, six rappels.

M   East Face

III   5.7 *(fig. 46) (photo, p. 141)*

Three tongues of snow (above the bergschrund) distinguish the lower E Face of the Central Tower. The middle tongue (more or less below the summit) marks the beginning of the route that wanders toward the central gully that leads to a notch in the summit ridge south of summit. **1–2** From snow tongue, scramble two pitches slightly left to base of steeper wall. **3–5** Climb one moderate pitch and continue working left (face-climb right around roof at base of book) to gain upper gully (open book), which is followed (right-facing corner) to summit ridge. Scramble ridge to summit; enjoyable climb. *Time:* 5–6 hours from bergschrund. *Descent:* Down-climb and rappel N Ridge or rappel S Ridge.

N   South Ridge

IV   5.8/A3 *(photo, p. 141)*

The route ascends the ice gully between the S and Central Towers to gain the proper S Ridge that is ascended to summit. First two pitches go up ice gully (70–75 degrees near top) on E Face to col (windy notch). From notch, climb obvious cracks (5.7/A3) to top of second step on ridge—can be done with clean aid, almost entirely with chocks. (High-standard free climbing might be possible.) At second step, traverse right onto E Face for final long pitch (5.8) to summit. *Time:* 6–7 hours from bergschrund. *Descent:* Rappel same route or down-climb and rappel N Ridge.

SOUTH TOWER

Approach: For the routes on the E Face, same as for the Central and N Towers. The best way to approach the S and W faces of the S Tower is via the Pigeon-Howser Col to East Creek Basin on the southwest side.

The most common descent off the S Tower is by rappel, down NE Face Route (five or six 160-foot rappels). First station located below summit on E Face (see photo, p. 141).

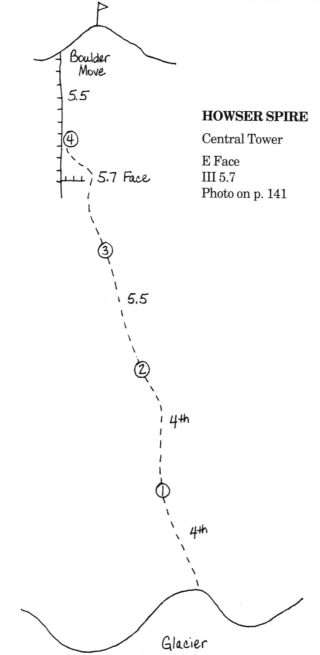

HOWSER SPIRE

Central Tower

E Face
III 5.7
Photo on p. 141

Fig. 46. Howser Spire, Central Tower E Face

O   East Face-Ridge

IV   5.6/A1 *(photo, p. 141)*

The prominent snow/ice slope on the lower south end of the E Face and corresponding ridge above the SE Shoulder characterize this route. Cross the bergschrund where it breaks toward the Pigeon-Howser Col and ascend down-sloping slabs on left side of snowslope or, alternately, crampon slope to shoulder. Traverse right on narrow ledge, then descend into rock-jammed couloir. Circle under patch of snow and cross slab to gain another gully filled with debris. Scramble gully and climb 25-foot crack to deep notch in E Ridge (150 feet above shoulder). Hand traverse out of notch via slanting crack to platform below short wall. Climb 15-foot pinnacle and follow scoop to bulge (A1). Three pitches to top, hardest ascends 50-foot slab via parallel cracks (5.6). About seven technical pitches of climbing. Although fewer technical rock pitches and more mixed climbing (ice/snow/rock), this route compares with SE Corner on Snowpatch. *Time:* 7–8 hours from Kain Hut. *Descent:* Rappel NE Face.

P   East Face Variation

(photo, p. 141)

Traverse under conspicuous snowpatch on E Face, adjacent shoulder and right of main snowfield. Climb two strenuous chimneys (5.8) to E Ridge. *Time:* Same as for E Face. *Descent:* Rappel NE Face.

Q   E Ridge Integral

IV   5.8/A1 *(photo, p. 141)*

From Pigeon-Howser Col, cross ice slopes and begin climbing E Ridge from lowest point. Climb steep chimney (5.6) to ridge crest. Ascend three pitches on broken ground (easy Class 5) to base of 140-foot slab. Climb cracks near left side (5.7), then overhanging chimney (5.8/A1). Two moderate Class 5 pitches lead to shoulder and original route. *Time:* 8–10 hours from Kain Hut. *Descent:* Rappel NE Face.

R   Northeast Face

IV   5.7/A2 *(photo, p. 141)*

A shallow trough descends in a plumb line directly from the summit to the bergschrund (now the normal rappel route off the S Tower). This is roughly the line followed by the first ascent party. Cross bergschrund and climb vertical left-facing crack/flake (A1); rappel to sloping ice-covered ledge (small hanging ice slope) and traverse right one rope length to huge cleft in face (150 feet above bergschrund). Loose rock initially, but when trough narrows, rock becomes excellent. Just below cleft, aid past ice patch, then lieback 125-foot pitch (good holds). Climb strenuous overhanging flake (A2, crux) and ascend slab/wall to right, then gully on left. Final slab-ramp leads to top. Exact number of pitches unclear. *Caution: some rockfall danger low on route.* **Time:** 7–8 hours from Pigeon-Howser Col. **Descent:** Rappel same route, 10 feet south of summit block (six double-rope raps, last of which is across bergschrund).

S   Big Hose Route

IV   *(photo, p. 141)*

The line follows the long (700-foot), distinctive 60- to 70-degree ice gully on the right side of the E Face. Strenuous, straightforward ice climbing with several 40- to 70-foot sections at 80 degrees. Upper one-third of route has crux chockstone (vertical ice when frozen). About 100 feet below summit, climb three short, blocky, narrow chimneys and surmount cornice to gain summit ridge. Enjoyable ice route when in condition. **Time:** 4 hours from bergschrund. **Descent:** Rappel NE Face.

T   North Face-Ridge

IV   5.6/A2

This route was originally done as part of the traverse of Howser Massif from the notch between the S and Central Towers and ascends the narrow N Face directly to the summit ridge. **1–5** Climb difficult pitches to easier ground. Climb several difficult but short steps to base of final crack (2–3 pitches). Climb final crack to easier ground and scramble to summit. Approximately 8–9 pitches. **Time:** 6–7 hours from notch. **Descent:** Rappel NE Face Route.

U   West Buttress/Beckey-Chouinard Route

V   5.10a *(fig. 47) (photo, p. 154)*

Approach: Descend the Pigeon-Howser Col into E Creek Basin. Traverse south and west (below S Tower Minaret) and descend another 1000 feet to gain toe of W Buttress. This very elegant route follows crest of long W Buttress (over 2500 feet of technical climbing). Scramble first 1000 feet of lower buttress to a large split boulder (three pitches below where buttress steepens). **1–3** Step right around boulder, lieback to an easy corner that leads to ledge where wall steepens. **4–5** Low-angle wall split by several cracks (wide crack on right easy, but must switch left for best line

Howser Spire Massif, S Face

through roof). Continue to uncomfortable belay; long pitch above leads to crest of buttress and huge low-angle inside corner. **6–8** Step right around arete and scramble to base of huge open book. Climb corner 250 feet (5.8) to top. **9–10** Scramble very loose, easy gully to comfortable ledge. Climb cracks to large sandy bivi ledge below "Great White Headwall" (very long pitch with much rope drag). **11–13** At left end of bivi ledge, ascend wide crack, then wide chimney (take right side) followed by moderate inside corner (5.10 variant follows cracks on left wall from top of pitch 12 to avoid squeeze chimney on pitch 14), belay at jammed blocks. **14–16** Climb corner and squeeze into strenuous chimney (difficult with pack) to gully full of loose rock. Follow gully, exit left

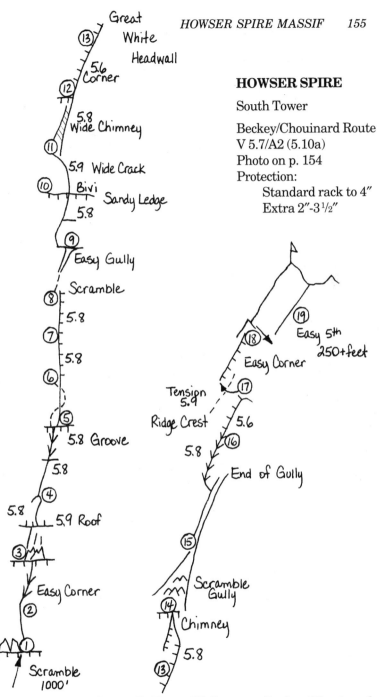

HOWSER SPIRE

South Tower

Beckey/Chouinard Route
V 5.7/A2 (5.10a)
Photo on p. 154
Protection:
    Standard rack to 4″
    Extra 2″-3½″

Fig. 47. *Howser Spire, S Tower W Buttress Beckey-Chouinard Route*

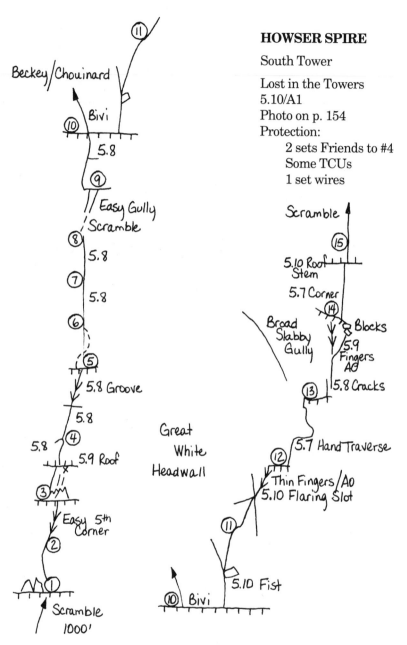

HOWSER SPIRE

South Tower

Lost in the Towers
5.10/A1
Photo on p. 154
Protection:
  2 sets Friends to #4
  Some TCUs
  1 set wires

Fig. 48. *Howser Spire, S Tower Lost in the Towers*

(fixed hex) to crack that leads to dihedral. **17–18** Ascend dihedral to top of pinnacle, then traverse left (tension or 5.9 +) across ridge crest and climb easy corner to notch in summit ridge. Rappel right from notch, climb and scramble (generally Class 4, 300 + feet) to summit. Classic strenuous crack climb. *Time:* 1–2 days from Pigeon-Howser Col. *Descent:* Rappel NE Face.

V   Variation: Lost in the Towers

5.10/A1 *(fig. 48) (photo, p. 154)*

Climb first 10 pitches of Beckey-Chouinard Route to sandy bivi ledge, then ascend cracks that split dramatic Great White Headwall. **11–12** From ledge, climb fist crack past protruding spike to sling belay; work right up flaring slot and thin finger crack (some easy aid). **13–14** Move right from belay and hand traverse to broad, slabby gully (poor rock). Step right out of gully into good cracks (one aid move), belay on sloping ledge above blocks. **15–16** Climb corner to roof, wild stemming past roof to easier ground. Scramble (Class 4) to summit. A committing and aesthetic variant. *Time:* 1–2 days from Pigeon-Howser Col. *Descent:* Rappel NE Face.

W   Catalonian Route

VI   5.10/A2 *(fig. 49) (photo, p. 154)*

Approach: Same as for Beckey-Chouinard Route. Route takes a direct line through a series of pinnacles or small towers to the summit several hundred feet south of the W Buttress. Ascend snow gully between W Buttress and Minaret to base of wall. **1–3** Start climbing 50 feet right of highest point of snow; ascend easy corners and cracks to base of dominant dihedral system. **4–6** Climb dihedral (sling belays). **7–9** Work left (some aid) and climb crack to easier ground and top of first tower. **10–13** Low angle terrain steepens toward left side of next tower (some aid). Follow left side to top of second tower. **14–16** Climb inside corner system (some aid) to where it is possible to move right. **17–20** Work right on easy Class 5 ground, then work left to ridge. Two more Class 5 pitches lead to top. *Time:* 2–3 days. *Descent:* Rappel NE Face.

SOUTH TOWER MINARET

X   West Face

V   5.10 + *(fig. 50) (photo, p. 154)*

Approach: Same as for Catalonian Route. Based on the original description of this route, the exact location is unclear. It is be-

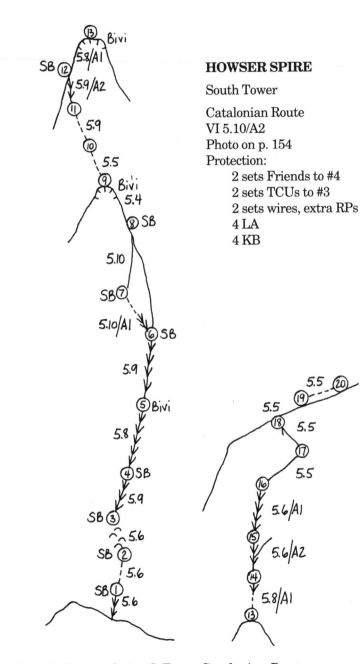

HOWSER SPIRE

South Tower

Catalonian Route
VI 5.10/A2
Photo on p. 154
Protection:
   2 sets Friends to #4
   2 sets TCUs to #3
   2 sets wires, extra RPs
   4 LA
   4 KB

Fig. 49. Howser Spire, S Tower Catalonian Route

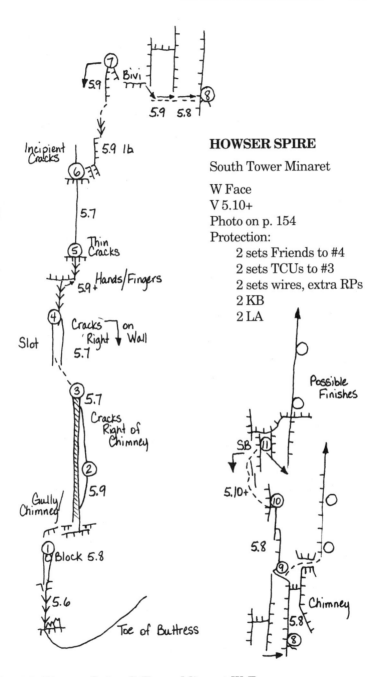

HOWSER SPIRE

South Tower Minaret

W Face
V 5.10+
Photo on p. 154
Protection:
    2 sets Friends to #4
    2 sets TCUs to #3
    2 sets wires, extra RPs
    2 KB
    2 LA

Fig. 50. *Howser Spire, S Tower Minaret W Face*

lieved that this unfinished route parallels the SW Pillar several hundred feet left (around the cone-shaped Minaret) and stops about 300 feet from the top of the Minaret. From the toe of the buttress, hike up and left next to the main face (near Catalonian start) until it is possible to scramble to good ledge with two rock spikes or horns. **1–3** Climb dihedral and chockstones in 10-foot-wide chimney. Scramble right on ledge (bushes on ledge) to gully/chimney, then climb to its top (use cracks on right wall, then back in main chimney). **4–6** Work left (good rock, abundant holds) to wide chimney (climb right wall). From horn, climb corner to roof. Climb right and follow shallow corner to ledge; good cracks fade at belay. **7–8** Work right (15–20 feet) to thin, intimidating flakes to horn. Down-climb east to ledge (good bivi), rap and traverse east past two corner systems to block. **9** Climb corner (first ascent party continued two more pitches to a dead end and rapped off, see suggested finishes on topo). Rock is superb and pitches offer interesting sequences of climbing, albeit strenuous. *Time:* 1–2 days from base. *Descent:* Rappel same route or continue to top of S Tower and rappel NE Face.

Y   South Face-Left/Italian Pillar

VI   5.10 + /A4 *(fig. 51) (photo, p. 154)*

Approach: Same as for Catalonian Route. Several thin crack lines split the main S Face of the Minaret; this route follows one that starts near the left side where a large slab has sheared away from the lower face leaving a sharp dihedral capped by a large angular roof. **1–4** Face-climb smooth slab to roof (hard aid). Continue up thin crack system beyond small roof on lower face to gain inside corner system. **5–8** Climb corner system (some aid) to top of small pinnacle (hanging bivi). **9–14** Continue up crack system two pitches above pinnacle, then scramble right (Class 4) to prominent crack system that is followed to top of Minaret. Ascend (Class 4) along Minaret ridge, then climb large gully to gain E Ridge and summit of S Tower (many Class 4 and easy Class 5 pitches). *Time:* 2 days or more. *Descent:* Rappel NE Face.

Z   Southwest Pillar

VI   5.8/A3 *(fig. 52) (photo, p. 154)*

Approach: Same as for Italian Pillar. Line ascends the obvious crack just right of inverted V-shaped roofs near base of pillar. **1–3** Aid thin cracks past roofs (difficult aid, thin) and pendulum into crescent-shaped crack. **4–9** Climb crack (mostly free) to triangular roof. Pass roof on right and continue along crack (free and easy aid) to top of tower (good bivi). **10–14** Move left at top of

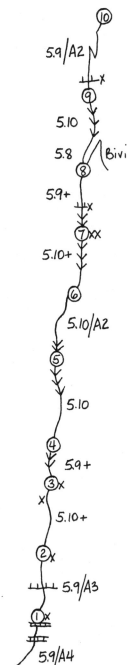

HOWSER SPIRE

South Howser Minaret

Italian Pillar
VI 5.10+/A4
Photo on p. 154
Protection:
    2 sets Friends to #4
    2 sets TCUs to #3

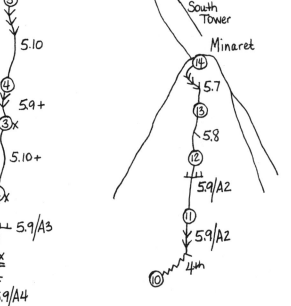

Fig. 51. *Howser Spire, S Tower Minaret S Face-Left Italian Pillar*

HOWSER SPIRE

South Tower Minaret

SW Pillar
VI 5.8/A3
Photo on p. 154
Protection:
  2 sets Friends to #4
  2 sets TCUs to #3
  2 sets wires, extra RPs
  6 KB, tie-offs
  6 LA

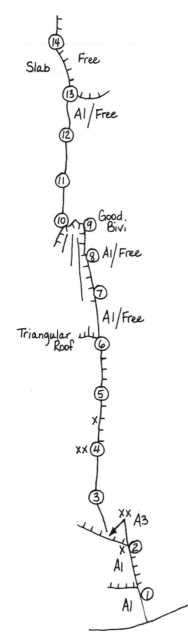

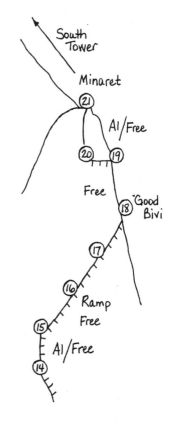

Fig. 52. *Howser Spire, S Tower Minaret SW Pillar*

tower and ascend single crack to slab and flake/corner (some easy aid). **15–18** Climb left-facing flake corner to right-slanting ramp. Follow ramp to good ledge (good bivi). **19–21** Free-climb crack to ledge. Traverse ledge left and climb crack to top of Minaret. Scramble (Class 4) along Minaret ridge, then climb large gully to gain E Ridge and summit of S Tower (many Class 4 and easy Class 5 pitches). Most aid is concentrated in lower 60 percent of route (thin, bottoming cracks); rock generally excellent, some bolts in place at belays. *Time:* 2–3 days. *Descent:* Rappel NE Face.

AA   South Face

V   5.8/A2

Approach: Descend Pigeon-Howser Col to base of main buttress. Route starts at foot of obvious fault, 200 feet left of toe of main buttress. Climb fault to top of pinnacle. **1–2** Climb to large ledge and traverse right past gully to crack system. **3–5** Climb this crack system to base chimney. **6–9** Climb left and then up chimney past roof (several points of aid) to sling belay; continue up crack system to finish via chimney on top of pinnacle. Exact location of route, and how first ascent party finished to summit unclear. *Time:* 1 day or more from Pigeon-Howser Col. *Descent:* Rappel NE Face.

MARMOLATA
9950 ft. (3032 m)
HOUND'S TOOTH
9250 ft. (2819 m)

Appearance and Location

These two spires split the Bugaboo Glacier into north and south forks. Hound's Tooth, the lower peak, is actually part of the larger, flat-topped peak, Marmolata, and a narrow saddle joins them. These two features are nunataks in the true sense—islands of rock surrounded by a sea of ice.

Although the peaks are aligned in a northeast-southwest direction, the faces and ridges are named after the main compass coordinates. Their northern slopes descend gently toward Pigeon

Spire and merge with the confusion of ice blocks and crevasses that characterizes the middle icefall on the north fork of the Bugaboo Glacier. Above the icefall, the glacier is a smooth expanse of neve, broken only intermittently by huge crevasses. The southern slopes drop steeply from the S faces of both peaks to the icefall of the glacier's south fork.

The receding glacier has revealed more of Marmolata's W Ridge, which descends steeply from the flat summit to the snow shoulder on the upper Bugaboo Glacier.

Notable First Ascent

Guides Conrad Kain and Peter Kaufmann led their client, Eaton Cromwell, up the easy northern snow slopes and scrambled the E Ridge to gain the untouched summit during the summer of 1930.

Climbing Marmolata and Hound's Tooth

Several routes have been established and all the major features exploited, but most present-day climbers only venture to these peaks as a diversion from the major Bugaboo Group. The rock is said to be of lesser quality, the major faces are often wet from snowmelt, and the approaches are arduous and can be dangerous due to crevasse danger and rockfall. These deterrents have confined most subsequent parties to the standard routes.

Most routes are mixed alpine experiences that are uncrowded and can be done in marginal weather, when it is impractical or unsafe to climb some of the other spires. Glacier excursions on the upper Bugaboo Glacier can be delightful experiences.

All the routes on the west, north, and so-called east sides are best approached via the N Fork of the Bugaboo Glacier from the Kain Hut. (Allow 1 to 2 hours for skirting the icefall and traversing the upper neve.) An alternate approach from a high camp at Bugaboo-Snowpatch Col or Pigeon-Howser Col can be accomplished by crossing Pigeon's W Ridge at its lowest point on the Vowell Glacier and traversing the upper N Fork of the Bugaboo Glacier. Routes on the south and southeast sides should be approached by way of the upper S Fork of the Bugaboo Glacier by crossing the W Shoulder of Marmolata. Allow an extra hour or more for approaches to this side of the peaks.

View from Kain Hut of the jumbled and broken North Fork of the Bugaboo Glacier; Hound's Tooth on the left and Marmolata on the right, with its head in the clouds

Route Descriptions

MARMOLATA

A East Ridge

II Class 4

Approach: Ascend lateral moraine above Kain Hut and skirt SE Shoulder of Snowpatch to gain upper N Fork of the Bugaboo Glacier. Traverse glacier above icefall to easy snowslopes of northern flank of peak. Ascend snow and follow ridge, best climbing generally on crest. Many variations exist. Climb short difficult step (15 feet) to gain flat summit. *Time:* 5 hours from Kain Hut. *Descent:* Rappel and down-climb W Ridge-N Face (one rap) or rappel and down-climb S Face-W End Variation (2 raps).

B Southeast Buttress

IV 5.3–5.4

Approach: Same as for E Ridge, except cross W Ridge at lowest point and circle to south. Route ascends right side of steepest yellow part of buttress. Climb tongue of snow to gain rock. **1–3** Climb easy cracks to roof. **4–5** Traverse right into narrow gully and climb until it widens (150 feet). **6–7** Climb dihedral (30 feet) and pass roof on right, then traverse left, descend 10 feet and stretch for holds to avoid another roof. Ascend steep slab to ridge and top. Route location and other details unclear, although first ascent party recommended the climb. *Time:* 7 hours from base. *Descent:* Rappel and down-climb W Ridge-N Face (one rap) or rappel and down-climb S Face-W End Variation (2 raps).

C South Face

II 5.5

Approach: Same as for SE Buttress. Route generally follows most prominent rib in center of face and ascends to the true summit. Ascend easy ground to wide talus-covered ramp halfway up face and between SE Buttress and W Shoulder. Climb left parallel crack to flake on left, then move to right crack to finish pitch. Stay right of rib; moderately easy ground (mostly Class 4) and two chimneys lead to top. *Time:* 2–3 hours from base. *Descent:* Rappel and down-climb W Ridge-N Face (one rap) or rappel and down-climb S Face-W End Variation (2 raps).

D South Face-West End

II 5.5

Approach: Same as for S Face and SE Buttress. Route ascends slabs and cracks diagonally up S Face to a point 200 feet below summit. Chimney through final white cliff band to top. *Time:* 4 hours from shoulder. *Descent:* Rappel and down-climb S Face-W End Variation (2 raps).

Variation: From shoulder, traverse diagonally up a broad ramp to couloir (filled with blocks) between SE Buttress and S Face Route. Scramble couloir to E Ridge at last 15-foot step on E Ridge Route.

E West Ridge-North Face

II

Approach: Same as for E Ridge, except traverse higher up glacier to base of wall. From W Shoulder, traverse east along ledges on N Face to about 150 feet below summit ridge. Ascend steep wall (unpleasant) to down-sloping slabs and ridge some 300 feet west of summit. Details unclear. *Time:* 1–2 hours from shoulder. *Descent:* Rappel and down-climb same route.

F North Face

II

Approach: Same as for W Ridge-N Face to large triangular snowfield below and slightly right of summit. Mixed climbing (ice/snow/rock) through broken ground. Traverse left 150 feet below summit to join E Ridge Route. *Time:* 1–2 hours from base. *Descent:* Rappel and down-climb W Ridge-N Face.

HOUND'S TOOTH

G Northwest Face

II Class 4

Approach: Same as for E Ridge, Marmolata. Work diagonally left up snowfield to gain easy rock rib. Scramble rock rib to summit. *Time:* 1–2 hours from glacier. *Descent:* Down-climb same route.

North Face Variation:

From the westernmost seracs of glacier, traverse east through seracs to base of N Face—*rockfall danger here* (crux is getting to start of route). Climb wet, mossy, debris-strewn rock angling left.

Finish in large right-facing chimney (5.6). Joins original route at top of snowfield on NW Face. Not recommended. *Time:* 2–3 hours from neve. *Descent:* Down-climb NW Face.

H   Northeast Side/Gilchrist-Raabe Route
III

Approach: Traverse icefall to east edge of steep snowfield arcing down from Hound's Tooth-Marmolata Col. Ascend snow and cross bergschrund on ledges on north slope. Traverse left to bottom of snowfield hanging above steep E Face. Climb four pitches of steep ice to top. *Time:* 3–4 hours from neve. *Descent:* Down-climb NW Face.

HOWSER PEAK
10,150 ft. (3094 m)

Appearance and Location

This massive snow-covered peak is the southernmost boundary of the Bugaboo Alpine Recreation Area. It is the highest point of Sextet Ridge, which includes the summits of Rock Ridge and Anniversary peaks. Its long E Ridge (Sextet) separates the N and S forks of Bugaboo Creek.

Notable First Ascent

The venerable Conrad Kain guided his friends, H. O. Frind, Albert and Bess MacCarthy, and G. and J. Vincent to its summit in 1916, in an east-west traverse of the ridge.

Climbing Howser Peak

This seldom-visited peak does not offer much technical climbing. The rock along the entire Sextet Ridge is different from that of the central Bugaboo Group, more akin to the sedimentary rock characteristic of the Rockies.

Route Descriptions

A   East Ridge
Class 4

Approach: Ascend S Fork of Bugaboo Glacier to snow col (9500 feet) east of peak. Climb ridge (mostly snow) to summit. *Time:* 6 hours from tongue of glacier. *Descent:* Down-climb same route.

B   Northwest Slopes

Class 3

Approach: Same as for E Ridge. Ascend easy snowslopes to summit (easiest route to summit). *Time:* 5 hours from tongue of glacier. *Descent:* Down-climb E Ridge or same route.

C   North Face-Right

Class 4

Approach: Same as for E Ridge or from Kain Hut via north fork of Bugaboo Glacier and W Shoulder of Marmolata. From bergschrund, west of summit under NW Ridge, ascend steep snow and scramble easy ground to summit. *Time:* 4–5 hours from Kain Hut. *Descent:* Down-climb same route.

D   North Face-Center

Class 4

Approach: Same as for N Face-Right. From bergschrund, ascend 50-degree snowslope between ice cliff on left and rock face on right. Rock is poor, and route is not advised. *Time:* 4–5 hours from Kain Hut. *Descent:* Down-climb same route.

FLATTOP PEAK
10,050 ft. (3063 m)

LITTLE SNOWPATCH
9550 ft. (2912 m)

CROSSED FISH PEAK
9350 ft. (2850 m)

Appearance and Location

Flattop Peak is about 1.5 miles southwest of Marmolata and 1.5 miles northwest of Howser Peak at the head of the Bugaboo Glacier. It is the head of a long, complex ridge that extends west and includes Little Snowpatch and Crossed Fish Peak.

The gentle northeast slopes are covered by the upper Bugaboo Glacier. Flattop's N and S ridges drop sharply to the west, however, revealing steep exposed walls.

Flattop's W Ridge descends gently to a saddle that separates it from Little Snowpatch and Crossed Fish Peak.

Little Snowpatch and Crossed Fish Peak stand isolated as they embrace the southern edge of the upper E Creek Basin. When viewed from the southwest side of Howser Spire, these two peaks have steep expanses of exposed rock along their lower ramparts. Only the ridge that connects them offers any easy access to their summits.

Notable First Ascents

The routes are all generally snow/ice walk-ups or very easy climbing.

Climbing Flattop Peak, Little Snowpatch, and Crossed Fish Peak

As this is written, no hard routes have been climbed on these peaks. Although they all offer an abundance of steep and compact granite, they have been largely ignored by climbers.

The approaches to the N and W faces are the same as for the W faces of Pigeonfeathers and the S and W faces of the Howsers. The upper Vowell or upper Bugaboo glaciers must be negotiated to descend into E Creek Basin via the Pigeon-Howser Col or by one of the many gullies on the west and southwest sides of Pigeonfeathers from Flattop.

Route Descriptions

FLATTOP PEAK

A   North Ridge

Class 3

Approach: From the upper Vowell Glacier cross the lowest point of Pigeon's W Ridge and traverse the upper Bugaboo Glacier; alternately, ascend the N Fork of the Bugaboo Glacier from Kain Hut to objective. Walk to summit. **Time:** 1 hour. **Descent:** Walk down same route.

LITTLE SNOWPATCH

B   West Ridge Slabs

Class 4

Approach: Descend from upper Bugaboo Glacier by way of Thimble-Howser Peak Col to small glacier below NW Flank of Flattop. Ascend notch between Little Snowpatch and Crossed

Fish Peak. From notch, ascend moderate slabs to summit. *Time:* 1 hour from notch. *Descent:* Down-climb to notch and descend rotten gully to south and regain upper Bugaboo Glacier via Thimble-Howser Peak Col.

CROSSED FISH PEAK

C   West Ridge

Class 4

Approach: Same as for Little Snowpatch. Traverse south, ascend snow couloir to col between Flattop and Crossed Fish peaks. Scramble 400 feet to top. *Time:* 2 hours from Bugaboo Neve. *Descent:* Down-climb and make one 150-foot rappel into notch between Crossed Fish Peak and Little Snowpatch.

APPENDIX A

Chronological First Ascent List

Key: Italicized name = Guide
      FA   = First Ascent
      FFA   = First Free Ascent
      FWA   = First Winter Ascent
      FFS   = First Free Solo
      AAJ   = *American Alpine Journal*
      CAJ   = *Canadian Alpine Journal*
      Inter/Rang = *Interior Ranges of Canada*

ROUTE NAME	NAME OF PARTY/DATE	REF.
EASTPOST SPIRE		
NE Ridge FA	E. Cromwell/F. S. North Aug. '38	AAJ 3:368
NE Summit FA	G. Engelhard/F. S. North *E. Feus* Aug. '39	AAJ 4:82
E Face FA	AA club members July '46	CAJ 30:154
Upper SE Ridge FA	M. Sherrick & party '55	AAJ 13:242
SE Ridge Direct (complete) FA	J. McKenzie/K. Mitchell *H. Gmoser* July '61	Inter/Rang 77:66
S Face FA	J. Kor/W. Sanders July '60	CAJ 44:83
S Face-Left FA	G. Campbell/S. Fuka/ P. Nelson/P. Zvengrowski July '67	AAJ 16:176
Shelton Route W Face	J. Shelton Aug. '74	
W Face FA	D. Perkins/B. McKown/Etman Aug. '75	
NW Ridge	Unknown	

APPLEBEE DOME

Dislocation	A. Thompson/L. Vanswam/	
FA	N. Paton/J. Weiss Aug. '71	

COBALT LAKE SPIRE

N Ridge	A. C. Faberge & ACC party	CAJ 36:99
FA	Aug. '46	
SW Face	M. Sherrick & party	Inter/Rang
FA	July '55	77:65

BRENTA SPIRE

S Ridge	L. Coveney/S. B. Hendricks/	AAJ 3:298
FA	P. Olton/P. Prescott/	
	M. Schnellbacher July '38	
N Ridge	D. P. & I. A. Richards	AAJ 3:369
FA	Aug. '38	

NORTHPOST SPIRE

N Ridge/NE Rocks	D. P. & I. A. Richards	AAJ 3:369
FA	Aug. '38	
NW Face	F. Beckey/G. Fuller	AAJ 15:375
FA	Aug. '66	
NW Face-W Side	J. Alt/S. Arsenault/V. Vogt	AAJ 16:175
FA	June '67	

CRESCENT SPIRE

SE Slopes	J. M. Thorington/C. Kain	AAJ 2:189
FA	June '33	
SW Gully	Unknown	Inter/Rang
		77:65
W Ridge	W. Brinton/H. Fuller/H. Gates	CAJ 26:18
FA	Aug. '38	
S Face-Right	J. Heron/R. Lofthouse	AAJ 16:414
FA	'68	
Woza Moya/	A. Long/D. Hoffman	

Right Dihedral FFA	July '73	
Surprisingly Subsevere (FFA variation of Woza Moza)	A. Lowe/E. Doub July '79	
S Face-Left Dihedral FA	B. Greenwood/R. Lofthouse '68	AAJ 16:414
Paddle Flake/ Left Dihedral Variation	Unknown	
NE Ridge	Unknown	Inter/Rang 77:66
McTech Arete FFA FFS	P. McNurtney/D. Klewin Aug. '78 P. Croft	
McTech Direct/ Variation Right FA	Unknown	
McTech Direct FFA	A. Lowe/E. Doub July '79	
Roof McTech FFA	A. Lowe/C. Bretherton July '79	
Energy Crisis FA	H. Herr/D. Peterson Aug. '80	
WIMTA FFA	D. Vachon/J. Moreland Aug. '83	

CRESCENT TOWERS
North Tower

N Ridge FA	E. Cromwell/G. Englehard Aug. '38	AAJ 3:369
NW Ridge- SW Gully-Right FA	A. & C. Damp '72	CAJ 36:73

Central Tower

Lion's Way	*H. Gmoser/*	Inter/Rang
FA	Mr. & Mrs. T. Hindset	77:66
	'68	

Tiger's Trail	C. Atkinson/J. Martinek	
FA	June '88	

South Tower

Ears Between	R. Lofthouse & CMC party	AAJ 16:414
FA	'68	

Thatcher Cracker	C. Kenyon/T. Fields	
FA	Aug. '86	

BUGABOO SPIRE

S Ridge/Kain Route	A. H. & E. L. MacCarthy/	CAJ 8:25
FA	*C. Kain* Aug. '16	

Gendarme Variation-Right	E. R. Gibson/R. C. Hind	CAJ 30:155
FA	July '46	AAJ 6:446

Gendarme Variation-Left	Unknown	

Variation	A. J. Kauffman/W. L. Putnam	Inter/Rang
FA	July '68	77:69

W Face	F. Beckey/P. Geiser/R. Sadowy	AAJ 12:23
FA	Aug. '59	

W Face Direct	E. Cooper/E. Pigou	CAJ 43:74
FA	Aug. '59	

NE Ridge	D. Craft/D. Isles/	AAJ 11:313
FA	R. D. Sykes/J. M. Turner	
	Aug. '58	
FWA	J. Buszowski/B. Ehmann '85	

Variation	L. F. Andrews/C. E. Fay	Inter/Rang
FA	July '63	77:71

N Face	L. Kor/C. Suhl	CAJ 44:82
FA	Aug. '60	

N Face Direct FA	W. Robinson/B. Ehmann	
E Face/ Cooper-Gran Route FA FFA	E. Cooper/A. Gran Aug. '60 M. Tschipper/T. Gibson Aug. '80	CAJ 44:77 AAJ 12:383
E Face-Left/Herr[2] FA	H. Herr/H. Herr Aug. '80	
Midnight Route FA	J. Wilson/P. Cole July '81	
Pretty Vacant FA	J. Buszowski/C. Thompson FA Aug. '83	

SNOWPATCH SPIRE

SE Corner (S Summit) FA	J. Arnold/R. Bedayn Aug. '40	AAJ 4:219
Variation FA (incomplete)	C. Cranmer/F. H. Wiessner July '38	Inter/Rang 77:72
Variation: Direct Finish FA	A. & C. Hall/C. Boeking Aug. '86	
Kraus-McCarthy Route FA	H. Kraus/J. McCarthy Aug. '56	AAJ 10:229
NW Corner/ Buckingham Route FA (N Summit)	W. Buckingham/A. Guess/ R. Page/E. Whipple July '58	AAJ 11:311 CAJ 42:53
Hudson-Gran Variation FA	A. Gran/J. Hudson Aug. '61	AAJ 13:242
Kruszyna-Andrews- Fay Variation FA	R. Kruszyna/L. F. Andrews/ C.E. Fay Aug. '63	AAJ 14:200
Beckey-Mather Route FA	F. Beckey/H. Mather Aug. '59	AAJ 12:17

Beckey-Greenwood Route FA	F. Beckey/B. Greenwood July '59	AAJ 12:21 CAJ 43:73
Gran-Hudson Route FA	A. Gran/J. Hudson Aug. '61	AAJ 13:242
S Face Direct FA	H. Abrons/G. C. Millikan July '65	Inter/Rang 77:74
S Face-Upper Section FA FFA	J. Hudson/A. Leemets/ R. Williams July '66 R. Rohn/T. Gibson '80	AAJ 15:283
Beckey-Rowell Route FA	F. Beckey/G. Rowell Aug. '67	AAJ 16:173
Variation: Right FFA	J. Gaskin & friend '77	Inter/Rang 77:75
S Face-Left FA	C. Jones/J. Lowe Aug. '71	CAJ 55:78
SW Ridge FA	B. Greenwood/G. Homer Aug. '71	CAJ 55:78
Variation: SW Ridge Direct Finish FA	E. Davies/P. Derouin Aug. '71	CAJ 55:78
E Face Diagonal FA	T. Chouinard/P. Carman/ D. Tompkins Aug. '71	CAJ 55:79
Bugaboo Corner FA	E. Davies/P. Derouin/I. Rowe July '71	CAJ 55:78
Degringolade FA	J. Jones/S. Hechtel '73	
Variation: Rock the Casbah FA	R. Atkinson/C. Thompson Aug. '84	
Wildflowers FFA	A. Higbee/B. Dougherty '74	

Banshee FFA	A. Higbee/M. Kosterlitz July '74	
Deus ex Machina FA	M. Jefferson/D. Sanders/ J. Shervais Aug. '74	AAJ 20:472
Variation FA	P. Littlejohn/D. Llato Aug. '76	
In Harm's Way FA	P. Cole/M. Richey/R. Rouner Aug. '75	
Sunshine Wall FFA	A. Higbee/D. Breashears '75	
Variation: Parker/Brashaw Route FA	A. Parker/P.R. Brashaw July '77	
Quasimodo FA	D. Nicol/E. Weinstein Aug. '75	
Flamingo Fling FA	R. Accomazzo/T. Sorenson '75	
Hobo's Haven FA (solo)	J. Boyer Aug. '76	
Tom Egan Memorial FA	D. Hatten/J. Simpson '78	
Variation: White Ducks In Space FA	R. Orvig/J. Richardson July '87	
N Summit Direct FA FFA	P. Morand/J. C. Sonnenuye Aug. '79 R. Rohn/T. Gibson Aug. '81	
Sunshine FFA	A. Lowe/S. Scott July '80	
Dark Side of the Sun FA	J. Simpson/J. Buszowski '80	

Furry Pink FFA	P. Croft/G. Foweraker '80	
Lightning Bolt Crack FA	G. Banks/L. Dean/N. Beidleman Aug. '81	
Tower Arete FA	R. Green/R. Gibbons/C. Hecht July '86	
Attack of the Killer Chipmunks FA	C. Thompson/G. Creighton Aug. '86	
Tam-Tam Boom-Boom Pili-Pili FA	J. Lemoine/P. Tanguy/P. Faivre Aug. '87	
Which Way Route FA	T. Thomas/C. Copeland Aug. '87	

PIGEON SPIRE

W Ridge FA	E. Cromwell/P. Kaufmann Aug. '30	AAJ 1:297
N Face FA	F. Beckey/J. Hieb/R. Widrig July '48	AAJ 7:134 CAJ 32:50
Miller-Shepard Route Var. FA	S. Miller/S. Shepard '61	Inter/Rang 77:87
Pigeontoe FA	D. Bernays/J. McCarthy July '54	CAJ 38:92
S Face FA	H. Kraus/J. McCarthy J. Rupley Aug. '56	Inter/Rang 77:89
E Face FA FFA	E. Cooper/L. Kor Aug. '60 E. Drummond/P. Buchanan July '74	AAJ 12:385 CAJ 44:75
Variation FA	R. Waslien/C. Martinson	
NW Face FA	F. Beckey/Y. Chouinard Aug. '61	AAJ 13:242 CAJ 45:127

SE Buttress FA	F. Beckey/S. Marts July '63	AAJ 14:199
SE Buttress Variation FA	D. Davis/G. Markov Aug. '72	
Feather Fallout FA	L. Johnson/R. Skelding/ S. Mikesell July '74	
Cleopatra's Alley FA	D. Knox/T. Thomas/ G. McCormick Aug. '87	
Tail-feather Pinnacle—Right Side FFA	J. Bensen/G. Klein/R. Green Aug. '87	
Wingtip FA	R. Green/C. Atkinson Aug. '87	
Parboosing Route FA	Parboosing/Lorentz July '88	
Lambice Tour FA	D. Ossola/G. Valenti/D. Deglise July '88	
Pigeontoe W Summit FA	D. Bernays/J. McCarthy July '54	CAJ 38:92
PIGEONFEATHERS W Peak FA	W. Briggs/P. Robinson Aug. '52	CAJ 36:99
E Peak FA	W. Doub/R. Irvin/G. Whitmore Sept. '53	CAJ 37:404

HOWSER SPIRE MASSIF
North Tower

E Face-S Ridge FA	H. O. Frind/A. H. MacCarthy/ E. L. MacCarthy/J. Vincent *C. Kain* Aug. '16	CAJ 8:20
E Face-N Ridge FA	C. Cranmer/S. B. Hendricks/ P. Olton/P. Prescott July '38	CAJ 26:23 AAJ 3:295
E Ridge-N Ridge FA	F. Ayres/E. Little/D. Woods/ J. Oberlin July '46	AAJ 6:447
N Ridge Integral FA	M. Finlay/E. Gale/ E. R. Gibson/T. Johnston/ A. Styles/D. Wessel July '46	CAJ 30:159 AAJ 6:447
W Buttress FA	F. Beckey/B. Greenwood Aug. '63	AAJ 14:198
NW Face FA	G. Campbell/W. Knowler/ P. Zvengrowski Aug. '67	CAJ 51:205 AAJ 16:174
SW Face FA	C. Jones/A. Simpson/ O. Woolcock Aug. '70	CAJ 54:76
W Face- Right/Seventh Rifle FA	C. Jones/G. Rowell/T. Qamar July '71	CAJ 56:73
W Face-Left/Warrior FA	H. Burton/M. Irvine/S. Sutton '73	CAJ 57:8
Mescalito FA	H. Burton/S. Sutton Aug. '73	
All Along the Watchtower FA	W. Robinson/J. Walseth Aug. '81	

Central Tower

N Ridge FA	G. Austin/D. Bernays/ J. McCarthy/J. Rupley Aug. '55	AAJ 10:105

S Ridge FA	B. Adams/J. Cameron/ D. Goeddel Aug. '72	AAJ 18:444 CAJ 56:73
E Face FA	A. Spero/D. Waterman Aug. '74	AAJ 20:150

South Tower

E Face-Ridge FA	L. Anderson/H. Beckey/ L. Boyer/T. Campbell Aug. '41	AAJ 4:421 CAJ 28:37
E Face Variation FA	W. Buckingham/P. Geiser Aug. '61	AAJ 13:243 CAJ 45:126
NE Face FA	F. Beckey/Y. Chouinard Aug. '61	AAJ 13:241
W Buttress/Beckey- Chouinard Route FA FFS FWA	F. Beckey/ Y. Chouinard Aug. '61 K. Trout June '77 P. Hein/S. Flavelle '82	AAJ 13:57
Variation: Lost in the Towers FA	W. Kamara/J. Walseth Aug. '80	
N Face-Ridge FA	Y. Chouinard/J. Lang/ E. Rayson/D. Tompkins Aug. '65	AAJ 15:39
E Ridge Integral FA	M. Heath/W. Sumner Aug. '70	CAJ 54:77
S Face FA	R. Mounsey/B. Beattie July '74	
Big Hose Route FA (Solo)	J. Krakauer '78	
Catalonian Route FA	J. Cabau/E. Burgada/ A. Masana/J. Wenciesko Aug. '83	

South Tower Minaret

SW Pillar FA	J. Jones/G. Rogan Aug. '72	CAJ 56:22
Minaret W Face FA	E. Doub/I. Stoble Aug. '79	
S Face-Left/ Italian Pillar FA	F. Stedile/F. DeFrancesco July '87	
Traverse Howser Massif N-S FA	Y. Chouinard/J. Lang/ E. Rayson/D. Tompkins Aug. '65	AAJ 15:38

MARMOLATA

E Ridge FA	E. Cromwell/*C. Kain* *P. Kaufmann* Aug. '30	AAJ 1:298
SE Buttress FA	J. Turner/M. Ward July '59	AAJ 12:135
S Face-W End FA	J.F. Brett & ACC party July '59	AAJ 12:135 CAJ 43:123
S Face FA	G. Fryklund, R. Kruszyna Aug. '60	AAJ 12:386
N Face FA	G.I. Bell/D. Michael Aug. '62	Inter/Rang 77:91
W Ridge-N Face FA	E. Gale/E. R. Gibson/ B. Hampsen/I. B. Kay/ J. McDonald/A. R. Styles/ D. Wessel July '69	CAJ 30:158

HOUND'S TOOTH

NW Face FA	L. Kor/W. Sanders Aug. '60	CAJ 44:83
N Face Variation FA	G. & H. Marinakis Aug. '82	

NE Side/ Gilcrest-Raabe Route FA	J. Gilcrest/P. Raabe Aug. '71	Inter/Rang 77:92

HOWSER PEAK

E Ridge FA	H. O. Frind/ A. H. & E. L. MacCarthy/ G. & J. Vincent/ *C. Kain* Aug. '16	CAJ 8:23
NW Slopes FA	E. Cromwell/*P. Kaufmann* Aug. '30	AAJ 1:298
N Face-Right FA	W. Buckingham/A. Guess/ R. Page/E. Whipple July '58	Inter/Rang 77:93
N Face-Center FA	E. Bjornstand/E. Cooper July '60	CAJ 44:74

FLATTOP PEAK

N Ridge FA	E. Cromwell/*P. Kaufmann* Aug. '30	AAJ 1:299

LITTLE SNOWPATCH

W Ridge Slabs FA	W. Buckingham/F. Garneau/ P. Geiser Aug. '61	AAJ 13:242

CROSSED FISH PEAK

W Ridge FA	W. Buckingham/E. Aston/ P. Garneau/P. Geiser/ S. Redpath Aug. '61	AAJ 13:242

APPENDIX B

Climb Rating Comparison Table

YDS	NCCS	British Numerical Pitch	British Adjectival
Class 1	F1		Easy (E)
Class 2			
Class 3	F2	1 a,b,c	Moderate (MOD)
Class 4	F3		
5.0			Difficult
5.1	F4	2 a,b	(DIFF)
5.2		2 c, 3 a	Very Difficult (V DIFF)
5.3	F5		
5.4		3 b,c	Mild Severe
5.5		4 a	Severe (S)
5.6	F6		Hard Severe
5.7	F7	4 a,b,c	Very Severe (VS)
5.8	F8	5 a,b	Hard Very Sev.
5.9	F9		(HVS)
5.10a			
5.10b	F10	5 b,c	Mild Extremely
5.10c			Severe (MXS)
5.10d	F11		(E1, E2)
5.11a	F12		
5.11b		6 a,b,c	Extremely
5.11c			Severe (XS)
5.11d	F13		(E3, E4)
5.12a			
5.12b			
5.12c		7 a	Hard Extremely
5.12d			Severe (HXS)
5.13a			(E5, E6)

BIBLIOGRAPHY

B.C. Ministry of Lands, Parks and Housing. Bugaboo Glacier Brochure.

Beckey, Fred. *AAJ*, Vol. 13.

Beckey, Fred. *AAJ*, Vol. 14.

Beckey, Fred. *AAJ*, Vol. 16.

Bedayn, Raffi. *American Alpine Journal*, Vol. 4.

Boss, Eugene. *Canadian Alpine Journal*, Vol. 59.

Burton, Hugh. *CAJ*, Vol. 57.

"Canada," *Mountain Magazine*, No. 11.

Cromwell, Eaton. *AAJ*, Vol. 3.

Garden, J.F. *The Bugaboos: An Alpine History*, Footprint, 1985.

Garden, J.F. *The Selkirks, Nelson's Mountains*, Footprint, 1985.

Greenwood, Brian. *CAJ*, Vol. 55.

Guess, Arnold. *CAJ*, Vol. 42.

Hudson, John and Williams, Richard. *AAJ*, Vol. 15.

Jones, Chris. *Climbing In North America*, AAC, 1976.

Kor, Layton. *CAJ*, Vol. 44.

Kruszyna, Robert and Putnam, William. *Interior Ranges of Canada*, AAC, 1977.

Morse, Randy. *Mountains of Canada*, Mountaineers, 1978.

North, Francis. *AAJ*, Vol. 3.

Rowell, Galen. *AAJ*, Vol. 18.

Thorington, James. *AAJ*, Vol. 2.

Wheeler, Arthur. *AAJ*, Vol. 1.

INDEX

ABOUT THE AUTHORS

Randall Green and Joe Bensen have been climbing together since 1979. Their climbing trips have taken them throughout the Cascades, to the Tetons, and, especially, to the Canadian Rockies and Bugaboos. They made their first trip together to the Bugaboos in 1980, and have not missed a summer since.

After his first visit to the Bugaboos, Green was so profoundly impressed with their magnificence and beauty, he convinced Theresa DeLorenzo to exchange wedding vows on the summit of Bugaboo Spire the next summer. Although the number of routes in the Bugaboos seem too numerous to climb in a lifetime, Green has climbed many of them and pioneered several new ones.

Green has written another guidebook, *Idaho Rock,* published by The Mountaineers in 1987. Currently, Green is finishing a bachelor's degree in journalism at the University of Montana.

Bensen interrupted a promising career as a ski bum and mountain tramp to pursue graduate studies in journalism and mass communication. He has a master's degree in photographic communication from the University of Minnesota, and is working toward a Ph.D. in the history of journalism.

Other books for climbers from The Mountaineers:

DEVIL'S TOWER NATIONAL MONUMENT: A Climber's Guide. Steve Gardiner, Dick Guilmette. Only complete, up-to-date guide to this monolith describes more than 140 routes, with ratings, equipment suggestions, and first-ascent data. Illustrated by photos with overlays. $10.95.

MEXICO'S VOLCANOES: A Climbing Guide. R. J. Secor. Approach and climbing routes for Popo, Ixta, Orizaba, others; information on food, medicine, transportation, supplies. Maps, photos, bilingual mountaineering glossary. $9.95.

CLIMBER'S GUIDE TO THE OLYMPIC MOUNTAINS, 3rd Ed. Olympic Mountain Rescue. Authoritative information on all access and climbing routes in the Olympics, plus winter travel and high-alpine traverses. $12.95.

CASCADE ALPINE GUIDE: Climbing and High Routes Series. Fred Beckey. Comprehensive climbing guide to Washington's Cascades. Sketches, photos with route overlays.
—Volume 1, 2nd Ed., Columbia River/Stevens Pass. $25.00.
—Volume 2, 2nd Ed., Stevens Pass/Rainy Pass. $25.00.
—Volume 3, Rainy Pass/Fraser River. $25.00.

HYPOTHERMIA, FROSTBITE AND OTHER COLD INJURIES: Prevention, Recognition, Pre-hospital Treatment. James A. Wilkerson, M.D. Experts describe symptoms, solutions and prevention. Includes immersion. $9.95.

MEDICINE FOR MOUNTAINEERING, 3rd Ed. James A. Wilkerson, M.D. The "bible" for travelers more than 24 hours away from medical aid and for climbing expeditions. $12.95.

ABC OF AVALANCHE SAFETY, 2nd Ed. E. R. LaChappelle. Classic guide to the basics--determining traveling safety in avalanche terrain, what to do if caught in an avalanche, search, rescue. $5.95.

Ask for these at your local book or outdoor store, or phone order toll-free at 1-800-553-HIKE with VISA/Mstercard. Mail order by sending check or money order (add $2.00 per order for shipping and handling) to:
The Mountaineers Books
306 2nd Avenue West, Seattle, WA 98119

Ask for free catalog